MARCO 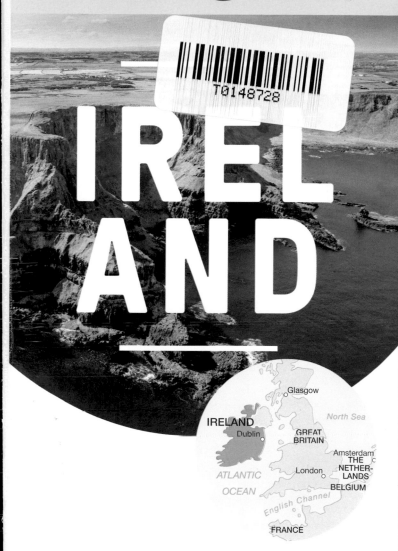 POLO

IRELAND

T0148728

Glasgow

North Sea

IRELAND
Dublin

GREAT
BRITAIN

Amsterdam
THE
NETHER-
LANDS

ATLANTIC

London

OCEAN

BELGIUM

English Channel

FRANCE

www.marco-polo.com

THE TOURING APP

shows you the way...
including routes and offline maps!

FREE!

GET MORE OUT OF YOUR MARCO POLO GUIDE

IT'S AS SIMPLE AS THIS

1 go.marco-polo.com/irl

2 download and discover

GO!

WORKS OFFLINE!

SYMBOLS

- INSIDER TIP — Insider Tip
- ★ — Highlight
- ●●●● — Best of...
- Scenic view
- Responsible travel: for ecological or fair trade aspects
- (*) Telephone numbers that are not toll-free

PRICE CATEGORIES HOTELS

Expensive	over 160 euros
Moderate	80–160 euros
Budget	under 80 euros

Prices are valid per night for two people in a double room with breakfast

PRICE CATEGORIES RESTAURANTS

Expensive	over 40 euros
Moderate	20–40 euros
Budget	under 20 euros

Prices are valid for a meal with starter, main course and dessert without drinks

 On the Cover: The spectacular Cliffs of Moher p. 76 | A pub crawl through Dublin p. 41

CONTENTS

DID YOU KNOW?
Timeline → p. 14
Local specialities → p. 28
Dog racing → p. 57
For bookworms & film buffs → p. 94
National holidays → p. 117
Currency converter → p. 121
Budgeting → p. 123
Weather → p. 125

MAPS IN THE GUIDEBOOK
(128 A1) Page numbers and coordinates refer to the road atlas
(0) Site/address located off the map
Coordinates are also given for places that are not marked on the road atlas
(U A1) Coordinates for the map of Dublin in the back cover

(🕮 A–B 2–3) Refers to the removable pull-out map
(🕮 a–b 2–3) Refers to the inset of the removable pull-out map

INSIDE FRONT COVER:
The best highlights

INSIDE BACK COVER:
City maps of Dublin, Limerick and Cork

The best MARCO POLO Insider Tips

Our top 15 Insider Tips

INSIDER TIP Take in the salty air

Experience the Cliffs of Moher (photo right) on a boat. This spectacular natural wonder is 200 m/656 ft high and home to many sea birds, like the Atlantic puffins, who live in secluded spots where the waves crash against the rocks below. You'll only be able to hear and see them on the water → **p. 76**

INSIDER TIP Peninsula in the rough Atlantic

Roughly 100 km/62 mi long, the *Ring of Beara* is a great alternative to the better-known (and oh, so busy) Ring of Kerry. The Beara Peninsula also boasts lush vegetation and a dramatic coastline → **p. 62**

INSIDER TIP Teatime in the park

Stop for lunch or afternoon tea at *Muckross Garden Restaurant* in Killarney. Its large terrace is unique, and boasts beautiful views of the old greenhouses as well as the manor house's Victorian landscaped park → **p. 60**

INSIDER TIP And the eagle flies...

Located in County Sligo, at *Eagles Flying*, you'll watch up close as birds of prey show off their flying skills → **p. 83**

INSIDER TIP A dreamy country home

A parkland filled with sheep. In the centre is a Georgian home called *Temple House,* and it's been home to the Perceval family for centuries. Helen and Roderick greet their guests with plenty of warmth and have many stories to tell → **p. 84**

INSIDER TIP Over Dublin's rooftops

Croke Park stadium is not just for playing Gaelic football – the *Skyline* tours take you up onto and around its roof → **p. 37**

INSIDER TIP A pub in the far west

Small, unpretentious and popular among Irish folk lovers, *Matt Molloy's Pub* in Westport is owned by Matt Molloy. He's been the flautist of the band *The Chieftains* for over 30 years → **p. 78**

INSIDER TIP Oyster beds

True to its original style, *Moran's Oyster Cottage* is a 300-year-old thatched building by the weir. If you're uncertain, the Fish & Chips are just as mouthwatering! → **p. 73**

INSIDER TIP Look to the stars

Once used to determine the temperature of the moon, this ancient *telescope* still works perfectly – get a closer look at Birr Castle → **p. 93**

INSIDER TIP Shopping in the manor house

Jams in Victorian terracotta pots, sugar rock in luminous colours: the products for sale at the *Avoca Store* in Powerscourt House are a visual treat → **p. 45**

INSIDER TIP By cable car onto the lonely island

Nothing for scaredy-cats: the dramatic 30 m/100 ft cable-car trip leads across the spectacular Dursey Sound to the rocky Atlantic islet of Dursey Island → **p. 62**

INSIDER TIP As pretty as a picture

Located along the Wild Atlantic Way heading towards *Dingle*, you'll find a peninsula with the same name – an unspoilt place in an unforgettable setting! → **p. 62**

INSIDER TIP Concerts in church

A full house in an old church? At *Triskel Christchurch*, now a cultural pillar, you'll see performances by both Irish and international musicians and artists → **p. 53**

INSIDER TIP Tapas served in style

At the *Market Bar,* you'll be able to enjoy Dublin over Irish drinks and seafood in an old, stylish factory. → **p. 40**

INSIDER TIP Amongst dolphins and seals

Captain Raymond Ross knows where to best observe marine mammals. Joining his *Seafari* guarantees a close encounter with nature and typically Irish humour (photo left) → **p. 114**

BEST OF...

GREAT PLACES FOR FREE
Discover new places and save money

● Irish Folk
Live music can be expensive, especially in Ireland. Some of the pubs in Dublin offer free entry. At The Brazen Head and The Temple Bar, they'd rather sell more beer than charge you an entry fee → p. 41, 42

● Old Masters
An oasis of calm and the arts, Dublin's National Gallery of Ireland is the place to enjoy European masterpieces and to have arts students guide you through the exhibition rooms – for free → p. 36

● James Joyce live!
In Sweny's Pharmacy in Dublin, where Leopold Bloom (main protagonist of 'Ulysses') purchased his lemon soap, you can browse through the volumes of poems, read literature journals, drink tea and listen attentively to inimitable readings → p. 38

● Local history in a contemporary setting
Housed in modern architecture on the banks of the Corrib, the Galway City Museum takes you on a journey into the past → p. 71

● Art at the customs house
The small charming *Crawford Art Gallery* in Cork is off the beaten tourist track. Enjoy the calm, stylish atmosphere, take in paintings and precious artefacts found in the region – no charge! → p. 49

● Street parades for St Patrick
On 17 March, as well as the days before and after, the *St Patrick's Festival* in Dublin lets you experience how the Irish celebrate their patron saint: with street parades, dance and colourful events (photo) → p. 116

● Art in neoclassical surroundings
Free of charge: at the *Royal Hospital* Kilmainham in Dublin, Ireland's largest neoclassical building, beautiful rooms are given over to the *Irish Museum of Modern Art (IMMA)* as well as an arts centre → p. 36

○○○○● Dots in guidebook refer to 'Best of...' tips

ONLY IN IRELAND
Unique experiences

● *Ireland's rough beauty*
To experience the wild side of Ireland, head for the Aran Islands off the west coast. Discover *Dun Aengus*, an Iron Age fort perched on the edge of a cliff above the Atlantic, buffeted by the wind for over 2500 years now (photo) → p. 74

● *Pubs: places of inspiration*
Ireland's greatest writers had a stool with their name on it, and Irish musicians played their first gig in pubs. The *Dublin Literary Pub Crawl* and the *Musical Pub Crawl* through the nightlife hub of Temple Bar allows you to follow in their footsteps → p. 41

● *Celtic high crosses*
Come real close to Celtic spirituality: the high crosses standing in the grounds of the ruined monastery of *Monasterboice* are the highest – at over 6 m/19.7 ft – and arguably the most beautiful in all of Ireland → p. 44

● *Gone to the dogs*
At the dog races, at the *Greyhound Stadium* in Cork, for instance, you sit next to betting harbour labourers and fishermen, students and housewives. Cheer on the greyhounds with them, and indulge in the passion of the common man, which today runs through all social levels → p. 57

● *Folk music with country folk*
Every year in August, folk music lovers meets at the *Fleadh Cheoil na hÉireann*. Do as the Irish fans do: make music and have a dance at the many small festivals in villages and small towns → p. 116

● *Garden delights*
For two weeks in June, garden owners who have come together under the *West Cork Garden Trail* umbrella open their gates, giving insights into the fantastical world of wildflowers, orchids, rhododendrons, tropical trees and Himalayan cedars → p. 57

● *Round tower in the ruined monastery*
Mystical Ireland: to admire the most beautiful of the country's nearly millennial freestanding round towers, head for *Glendalough*. The tower belongs to the crumbling monastic settlement of the same name, one of the most mysterious places in the country → p. 44

ONLY IN

BEST OF...

● *Light at the end of the tunnel*
You won't get wet diving into the mystery of the megalithic tomb of *New-grange*. Once arrived at the heart of the passage tomb, some 5000 years old, an artificial ray of light demonstrates what happens naturally at the winter solstice (photo) → p. 44

● *Stay with the Count*
Breathe in Irish history in the beautiful, charmingly dusty family seat of the Earls of Bantry. Stroll through the salons of *Bantry House* and check out the family treasures at your own pace → p. 55

● *Dead Poets Society*
In the *Dublin Writers Museum*, you are right inside the universe of literary Dublin: even the waistcoat of James Joyce is exhibited here. And the in-house bookstore is a treasure trove for out-of-print books by Irish authors → p. 35

● *Dining medieval-style*
At a banquet at historic *Bunratty Castle*, you are a guest of the Middle Ages. Damsels entertain with ethereal song, the table is laden with hearty meat dishes and mead → p. 69

● *What a fine maze!*
Shopping in the historic town palace and the roofed-over atrium: meet Dublin's bohemian crowd in the exclusive shops, trendy cafés and restaurants of the *Powerscourt Centre* → p. 40

● *Going underground*
A worthwhile descent: over the course of two million years, nature has shaped *Aillwee Cave* into a massive cave maze with countless stalagmites, stalactites and a subterranean waterfall → p. 75

RAIN

RELAX AND CHILL OUT
Take it easy and spoil yourself

● *Trotting through the park*
Take a jaunt through *Killarney National Park* in a horse-drawn carriage to romantic places on the lake. On cooler days, plaid woolly blankets will keep you warm; the drivers will keep you entertained any day (photo) → **p. 58**

● *Seaweed in Sligo*
Irish algae have been rediscovered as a source of true rejuvenation: bathe in them or have a massage with hot herbal bags or hot stones at the *Voya Seaweed Baths*. Here, the traditional healing powers of the sea are combined with a good dose of design and zeitgeist → **p. 84**

● *Teatime in the terrace café*
The terrace café in the pretty landscaped park of *Powerscourt Gardens* affords views of fountains and sculptures that are best enjoyed with an Irish coffee and an apple pie fresh out of the oven, with a dollop of clotted cream → **p. 45**

● *Enlightenment included*
In a prominent position above the steep coastline of the Beara Peninsula, the Tibetan Buddhist *Dzogchen Beara* Centre welcomes anybody for daily meditation classes or retreats lasting a weekend or longer → **p. 62**

● *Cocktail in Killarney*
You won't find a more beautiful place for a sundowner in all Killarney than on the terrace of *The Europe Hotel & Resort*. The lake and mountains seem within your grasp → **p. 61**

● *Yoga by the sea*
Nobody is too old or too unfit to stretch their limbs at the *Burren Yoga Centre* near Kinvara. The place has not only a friendly atmosphere but also – according to New Age followers – a strong force field → **p. 75**

● *Cuisine at the cottage*
1826 Adare is a thatched cottage serving savoury food, but save room for dessert! Will you take the caramel parfait or chocolate pudding? → **p. 69**

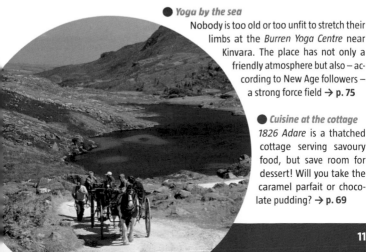

DISCOVER IRELAND!

In Ireland, many a small chat begins with a standard subject: the *weather*. But when the locals ask, *'Isn't it a nice day today?'*, this isn't just a good way to start a conversation; it also shows how resilient the Irish are – they'll even hail a gloomy, cloudy morning as a great day! No wonder the school kids wear knee socks and skirts during the cold winter months on the Emerald Isle. And besides, according to the country's pragmatic wisdom, with changeable weather come many advantages as well. And no matter how bad it gets, it never rains in the pub! The weather is so important in fact, the Irish have unique words to differentiate between the raindrops and wind. The weather forecast, for example, has dozens of rain names, like 'fine scattered drizzle' – an expression that just needs one word in Irish. But it's the rain that makes Ireland so beautifully green.

Ireland has a unique natural landscape. The island sits in the sea off the northwest coast of Europe like a moss-covered rock and boasts *wind-buffeted coasts, barren high plateaus* and *lush vegetation*. Anyone driving or cycling along the island's occasionally rutted and narrow roads will come to understand the song *forty shades*

Remnants of the Christian past: The monastic ruins of Glendalough

of green. It's anything but cliché. The rainfall and the sunshine interchange so often here that rainbows are no longer a rare occurrence.

Like the weather, Ireland's economic situation has also changed a lot over of the past few years. While Ireland was considered the *poorhouse of Europe* up to joining the EU in 1973, from the mid-1990s onwards, the country experienced an economic boom, earning it the epithet of Celtic Tiger and making it one of the wealthiest countries in the EU. Since 2008 things have been going downhill again, and fast. In early 2011, Ireland needed an EU cash injection of billions. Drastic austerity measures were imposed, and in return, this tense situation got better. Ireland is now thriving again and seeing massive *Growth*. Economically speaking, the Emerald Isle is once again a European champion! But ever since the 2016 *Brexit* vote, the country has been back on tenterhooks as the free border to Northern Ireland is at risk of being closed again. To-

400 BC–2nd century AD
Celts come to Ireland from Spain, forming small kingdoms. Trade with Britannia and Roman Gaul leads to Christianisation

8th century
Christianity spreads across the whole country, schooling is introduced, religious leaders obtain equal standing to secular rulers

1534
Henry VIII, King of England, subdues Ireland in the Battle of Maynooth

1845
Potato blight and harvest failures lead to famine. A million people die, another million emigrate

day, around 20,000 Northern Irish People commute to their jobs in the Republic of Ireland. Lorries and delivery trucks are constantly crossing over the border freely. This is the freedom many fear losing. Thankfully, however, the 1998 Good Friday Agreement has has helped ease people's minds. Not only did it put an end to 'The Troubles', a bloody, decades-long conflict, but it also officially renounced British jurisdiction over Northern Ireland. Although there's still reason to worry, the Irish are no people to let this political debate go and ruin their day.

The Irish are clearly enjoying the present economic boom. In the capital city, for example, vacant factories have become *creative workshops*. Once dismal districts are now buzzing with life, and new boutique hotels, clubs and *beloved gastropubs* are opening up everywhere. The gastropubs are bringing both bankers and students together for drinks while sports are bringing people even closer together. The Irish especially love playing golf – a sport that on the island is not the least bit elitist. *Pitch and putt*, a mini version of golf, is also popular. Ireland offers hundreds of golf courses, most of which boast lush, green vegetation. Many of these courses also offer a view over the roaring sea and dramatic cliffs.

A passion transcending generations and social class is betting. A high number of Dubliners name *greyhound races* as their favourite pastime. The evening events of the dog racetrack of Shelbourne Park attract a throng of young and old, men in corduroy suits and flat cap, youngsters in baggy tracksuit bottoms and top-dressed women accompanied by their female friends. Only a few decades ago, horse races and betting were considered the domain of the wealthier section of society, while dog races

1916
The Sinn Féin ('We Ourselves') party proclaims an Irish parliament. England replies with armed force; formation of the IRA

1921
Ireland is partitioned

1969
Violence between Protestants and Catholics in Northern Ireland, more British troops are sent, the IRA supports the Catholic defence

1973
Ireland joins the EC (European Community)

2002
Introduction of the euro

were associated with the working class. There is another tradition that has survived: the favourite pastime of many rural women remains *bingo*.

What makes Ireland so endearing, alongside the open and outgoing people, is the country's *natural beauty*. The island boasts countless prehistoric and medieval cultural treasures: mystic places imbued with power. Towering *Druid stones* stand alongside ancient tomb chambers as well as ruins of nameless *castles from Norman times*. Amongst the extraordinary prehistoric survivals is Dun Aengus, a stone fort on the Aran Islands, as well as a burial chamber in Newgrange in Co. Meath that is around 5000 years old. Every year on 21 December a magical light show is revealed when the rays of the sun enter the passage through a cunningly constructed opening. Early Christianisation left its traces in high crosses, round towers and monastic complexes. Thus an important monastic settlement formed around the year 1000 in Glendalough (Co. Wicklow), while the Gallarus Oratory on the Dingle Peninsula dates to the 8th century.

> **An old burial chamber boasting a magical light show**

At the most beautiful spots of the country, British nobility once built their mansion houses, beautiful *country estates* which over the course of time appeared to fuse with the landscape around. Typical are the entrance portals surrounded by climbing ivy and vines, their tall lattice windows, quarry-stone mews and turreted gatehouses, as well as the Victorian-style conservatories. Many of the castles, manor houses and fortified houses today open their gates to a paying public, or serve as restaurants or hotels. The interior is usually original: fireplaces as tall as a man, wood-panelled libraries, gently curving staircases, as well as rooms furnished with antiques.

A trip to Ireland is also an encounter with a different concept of time. 'When God made time, he made enough of it', would sum up the approach of a lot of Irish people. All it means is: *take it easy*. For instance when the boat service to one of the small islands can only run again the following day, or when those drops start to fall and the planned excursion is literally rained off. Ireland is particularly beautiful in the spring, when huge rhododendrons, extensive fuchsia groves and deep-green pastures

2005 Changeover to the metric system

2007 After 38 years, the British army ends its deployment in Northern Ireland

2010 Ireland narrowly escapes state bankruptcy

2014 Ireland is the first of the EU crisis countries to leave the safety net

2017 Leo Varadkar becomes taoiseach (prime minister)

gleam in the sun. Bird colonies nest along the steep coastline, the magic of the light defying description. The western coast attracts most visitors. 2500 km/1553 mi long, the route called the *Wild Atlantic Way* offers mind blowing views. It's also the *world's longest marked coastal street* and the most beautiful to boot! It's the latest craze in Irish tourism, and the views of the cliffs are enough to take your breath away. The trail goes from the southern fishing village of Kinsale and winds along the Atlantic coast up to Malin Head on the northern tip of Ireland. Take note that the roads are narrow and full of twists and turns, so travelling at high speeds is simply impossible. It's better to take things slow. While on the frayed western coastline, expect to visit places

Dolphin watching in Dingle Bay: Experience nature like never before!

with charming simplicity: A few dozen candy-coloured thatched cottages. A tiny grocery. A few pubs. *Men with flat caps* and weather-worn faces sit inside, talking with a hard accent and *knocking back pint after pint*. Harbours covered with lobster traps and surrounded by boats. The sound of the seagull's cry fills the air while (as the Irish say) *fuckin' poffins* steal the fishermen's hard-caught fish, and the mix of rain and sunshine make for rainbow-covered skies. You may ask yourself what the strange language is printed on the bi-

> **The seagull's cry and candy-coloured thatched cottages**

lingual sign posts. This is one of the EU's 24 official languages: Irish. Rooted in Celtic antiquity, it's a unique tongue. *An tAontas Eorpach*, for example, means 'European Union'. You'll find it in Irish passports printed in small print. Ask someone in the pub to show you – the Irish love their language. If you visit the pubs, one word that's especially important to know is 'cheers'. Just say, *Sláinte*!

WHAT'S HOT

1 Wellness from the sea

Active health bomb Seaweed is the island's natural wellness weapon. The plant's iodine content can be 20,000 times higher than in seawater, lending it a particularly high therapeutic force. During a *Voya Herbal Bag Massage*, the *Monart* health farm *(The Still | Enniscorthy | Co. Wexford | www.monart.ie) (photo)* wraps its spa guests in a blend of herbs and seaweed. Seaweed baths reclaim a traditional Irish custom – bathing with seaweed in hot seawater was a popular pastime centuries ago.

Gaelic football

2

Irish national sport Gaelic Football spans tradition and trend with ease. Tens of thousands of fans follow the ball being kicked and thrown at the *Croke Park Stadium (Jones Road | Dublin) (photo)*. The sport combines the velocity of football with the toughness of rugby. The fun is organised by the *Gaelic Athletic Association (www.gaa.ie)*. To find out all you need to know about the sport head for the *GAA Museum* at Croke Park *(St Joseph's Av. | Dublin | www.crokepark.ie/gaa-museum)*.

Movie Mania

3

Eldorado for cinema lovers Statistically, more people go to the cinema in Dublin than in any other city in Europe. Currently, independent Irish films are all the rage. *Filmbase (Curved Street | Dublin) (photo)* supports film-makers with material, studios and workshops. The *Irish Film Institute (6 Eustace Street | Dublin | www.ifi.ie)* also contributes to the current trend with small and bigger film productions and two screens. The *Lighthouse Cinema (Smithfield/Market Square | Dublin)* could be described as *hygge*. Enjoy their great seats and sophisticated films while sipping on red wine or a cup of tea!

Irish Taste

A new look for an age-old drink Compressing the calf muscles with whiskey? This odd health practice is long-outdated but was popular back when the monks invented *uisce beatha,* or 'water of life' in Irish. Today, along with Guinness, whiskey, a drink loved by the Irish, is no longer the gentry's nightcap – it's the *drink du jour*! Irish youth meet for *whiskey tastings* to taste the different flavours and discuss their level of enjoyment. New distilleries are opening up, too, like the successful *Teeling Distillery (www. teelingdistillery.com)* in Dublin. It's the only one to have opened along the River Liffey in the past 100 years. *Roe & Co* is another big name. Their premium blended whiskey has been on the market since 2017 and is pure enjoyment, especially when mixed in cocktails.

Gourmet boom

Cookery classes in the country The Irish discovered haute cuisine abroad and brought it back home with them. Now, the creation of fine dishes is booming on the Emerald Isle, with gourmet trips and cookery workshops becoming ever more popular. The most famous place to learn is *Ballymaloe Cookery School (Shanagarry | Co. Cork | www.cookingisfun.ie)* with its own 🌿 organic farm. The smallest cookery school is situated on idyllic Heir Island. Over two days, two participants learn the secrets of the kitchen at the *Island Cottage Cookery School (Skibbereen | Co. Cork | www.island cottage.com) (photo)*. The *Pangur Bán Cookery School (Letterfrack | Co. Galway | www.pangurban. com)* in Connemara boasts a spectacular location between the Atlantic and the Twelve Bens mountains.

IN A NUTSHELL

A GREEN MASTERPIECE

The mild Irish climate, favoured by the warm Gulf Stream and frequent short rain showers, ensures unique vegetation. It's true that Ireland resembles a massive landscape park, but many of the Irish have also turned their private gardens into horticultural gems, which they present to the public. Alongside generously laid-out cottage gardens, enchanted monastery gardens and Zen oases, you'll discover cool sculpture parks and so-called *fermes ornées* combining agriculture and horticulture. The latter shelter livestock threatened with extinction and grow heirloom vegetables, such as Larchill Arcadian Garden in County Kildare *(www.larchhill.ie)*. For an in-depth description of publicly accessible gardens, see *www.hcgi.ie,* for private gardens, also sorted by county, *www.garden.ie*.

A trend imported from Britain is the enthusiasm for organised garden tours lasting several days (e.g. through *www.essenceofireland.co.uk*). RTE One, the island's oldest TV channel, produces one garden programme after the other. For a beautiful coffee-table book look no further than 'The Gardens of Ireland', where British garden photographer Melanie Eclare presents 20 extraordinary gardens and their owners.

B ONO AND FRIENDS

The Irish have music running through their veins, and the list of top musicians with Irish descent is impress-

A Jedi island, a singles market, hardcore football, traditional folk, rock 'n' roll and a whole lot of green – Welcome to Emerald Isle!

ively long. Founded in 1962, The Dubliners are now legends in Ireland. That same year, five musicians got together and created a folk band called The Chieftains and are also still successful today. Bono, the lead singer of the Dublin-based rock band U2, has been leading the Irish pop music scene since 1976. Van Morrison, a Belfast-born jazz, blues and folk singer, is adored on a worldwide level. Then there's Bob Geldof, the lead singer of the Boomtown Rats; the folk-punk band The Pogues; and the female singers Sinéad O'Connor and Enya. Together with the boy bands Boyzone and Westlife, these artists make up Ireland's modern music scene. But the next generation is in the process of creating a new music scene. The Script, for example, after releasing the songs on their album 'Freedom Child', quickly made it onto the international charts.

DATING IN IRISH

Would you prefer speed dating or perhaps just going to the *Matchmaking*

Festival in the small town of Lisdoonvarna? It lasts about six weeks in the middle of the Burren which is a stone desert near Galway. Each September, tens of thousands of singles coming from Cork and Connemara travel here to find their match. There are even some Irish emigrants who travel all the way from Chicago or Cleveland to attend the festival. Day and night, visitors are entertained by fiddling folk bands while singles dance, share drinks, sweet-talk each other and, if the feeling's right, come a bit closer. If there's a single farmer who's better at milking cows than talking to women, they send him over to Willie Dally. He's been a successful matchmaker for over 50 years. During the festival, he moves his office into the Matchmaker Bar next to Imperial Hotel. And, since even Ireland is keeping up with the times, in the last week of the festival, the gay communities throw massive parties and put on drag performances.

INTERNATIONAL MASTERS OF DRAMA

The Irish don't just enjoy telling stories, they're masters at putting them down on paper. The land of poets and writers, Ireland can boast four Nobel Prize winners for literature: William Butler Yeats received it in 1923, Bernard Shaw in 1925, Samuel Beckett in 1969 and Seamus Heaney in 1995. Other Irish writers are no less famous: Jonathan Swift, Sean O'Casey, Oscar Wilde, Brendan Behan, Flann O'Brien and James Joyce. The last-named became famous with his Dublin novel 'Ulysses'. Published in 1918, it's still considered a groundbreaking piece of modern literature. Currently, Anne Enright, John Banville and Colum McCann garner the highest literary accolades. Irish novels and plays deal with idealism and humanity, ranging stylistically between emphatic poetry and often-subtle satire.

The James Joyce's statue in Dublin: A great writer immortalized

Peat briquettes in the moor at Connemara: A natural resource with tradition

INTO THE WILD

Managed by the 'National Parks and Wildlife Service' (NPWS), six national parks are home to many rare animals in Ireland. Here, golden eagles and Ireland's largest herd of red deer can roam wild. Glenveagh National Park *(www.glenveaghnationalpark.ie)* with its bogs, lakes and forests spanning over 155 km²/60 sq mi is the country's largest and most fascinating national park. It is located in the Derryveagh Mountains in County Donegal. In 1983, the park's former owner Henry McIlhenny handed over the land with its beautiful lakes and mountains to the Irish State. Now a public park, its visitor centre is at the northern end of Lough Veagh, and the hiking trails are particularly inviting!

IRELAND'S PERFUME

The smell of peat lingers above the villages of Ireland, rising up from the distant bogs and flames. At the start of the 19th century, 15 per cent of Irish land was covered with peat bogs. Traditionally, peat was mined and cut by hand. In 1946, the company *Bord na Móna* was established and now operates a peat power plant. Many of these peatlands have become nature reserves, including the 10,000-year-old Clara Bog in County Offaly which is 7 m/23 ft in depth.

MAY THE FORCE BE WITH YOU!

No wonder this sentence is known by everyone in Portmagee, a village opposite *Skellig Michael* (see p. 64). Luke Skywalker himself, the hero in 'Star Wars', poured himself a pint at the *Bridge Bar* where the entire crew celebrated after they finished shooting. The big ending in episode seven, lasting only three minutes, took place just 7 km/4.3 mi from the village's coast on a remote Irish island called Skellig Michael. Found at a most inaccessible location, dramatic cliffs make up the little island's landscape. In the Early Middle Ages, monks used it as a retreat and built a monastery on its peak. But Hollywood has now turned it into the retreat of a Jedi – lonely he abides here in the universe, patiently awaiting his end. After episode seven was shot, no one expected they'd be back on Skellig Michael for *Star Wars: Episode VIII – The Last Jedi*. The people of Portmagee are still in shock.

MUDDY FIGHTS AND BLOODY SHINS

Every September, when the all-Irish, Gaelic football finale takes place at Croke Park Stadium, there's never an empty seat in the house. When the Irish picture their sport heros, they see men with mud-covered arms and faces. The game is basically a mix between football and handball, but with a pinch of rugby on top.

If you really want to understand how the Irish tick, visiting the stadium at least once is an absolute must, for Gaelic football is hands down the most beloved sport on the island. It's filled with punching, pushing and shoving and makes football look like a bunch of senior citizens dilly-dallying on valium. It's hardcore and fast paced. The players are all professional amateurs but have to stay in the best of shape. And them being transferred over to another club is unheard of. None of these guys would ever let themselves be headhunted. This is another reason why their fans look up to them. A true fan would never dare miss their team play. If they do, they better start preparing their tombstone!

ON EVERYONE'S LIPS

Imagine you had a family recipe that was passed down from grandma. You enter it into a baking competition and win! Soon after, your bread is being sold at discount stores nationwide. For Phyllis McGovern, the owner of a small B&B in County Waterford, this dream became a reality. Of course, we're not talking about any bread here, we're talking about the famous Irish soda bread. Its taste and texture are similar to cake and you can eat it anyway you like. The Irish enjoy it with butter and jam in the morning and with salmon in the evening. Never tried it? Why not make it yourself! To Phyllis, it's as easy as pie. You just need wholemeal, wheat bran, oats, buttermilk and baking soda. The secret is – shh, don't tell! – crushed chia seeds. The jury of the National Brown Bread Baking Competition was simply blown away by its taste: 'Not too sweet. Not too heavy and hardly any crumbs'. Today, 'Phyllis's Brown Bread' can be found on the shelves at any Aldi store in Ireland. Sold at just 1.59 euros a loaf, it's a great deal!

SADDLE UP!

Ireland is a paradise for horse lovers, and not only because the island boasts the most beautiful riding trails and places for cantering. Three very popular breeds are native to the island: Irish Hunters are a cross between a thoroughbred and the Irish Draught horse; the robust Irish Tinker (originally a work and draught horse used by the Irish itinerant population) are considered excellent hunting and eventing horses, and Connemara ponies are particularly agile. Every year in October, horse lovers from all over the world make the pilgrimage to the Midlands, to Ballinasloe, for Europe's oldest and biggest horse fair – with funfair and tournaments *(www.ballisnasloeoctober fair.com)*.

ST SNAKE CHARMER

Ireland's patron saint represents the most important figurehead of Irish Catholicism – which is why the most common name in Ireland is Patrick (Paddy). Born around 385, probably in Wales,

Patrick was taken by force to the Emerald Isle by pirates around the year 400. Fleeing to France, Patrick joined the priesthood and returned to Ireland in 432 as a missionary. Using the tripartite shamrock, Patrick explained the Holy Trinity to the Irish. The Croagh Patrick mountain, on whose summit the saint is said to have fasted for 40 days in 441, banishing all snakes to the sea, became a place of pilgrimage. On 17 March 461, Patrick died in Northern Ireland. To this day, that date is commemorated as the Irish national holiday St Patrick's Day – with exuberant parties and parades.

THE MIRACLES OF KNOCK

Commonly called foggy-boggy, the small village of Knock in County Mayo is a place where miracles are said to have happened. The first was back in August 1879 when some locals witnessed an apparition of the Virgin Mary. Only a few pilgrims saw it and reported miracles of healing. The second miracle started with Monsignor James Horan who was on a passionate mission to turn Knock into an international pilgrimage site. In 1976, he and 10,000 other believers built a Basilica from the ground up. After construction had ended, he invited Pope John Paul II to visit the Knock Shrine in 1979. Soon after, a new construction site opened. Spades and bulldozers worked the site to build an airport where the pilgrims could arrive. The government issued the workers a building permit and the donations came pouring in. After construction, pilgrims flew in from all over the world. And now? Even you can fly into *Ireland West Airport Knock*. Upon arrival, Monsignor Horan will welcome you with open arms! His bronze statue shines triumphantly under the sun. He was a simple priest, yet next to the Virgin Mary, he symbolises Knock's second miracle.

TRAD SESSIONS WITH BAGPIPES

For traditional Irish folk fans, the Fleadh Nua Festival has become a yearly ritual, taking place in the small town of Ennis each summer. In the town's pubs, the island's best musicians agree to meet for a pint of stout and a so-called trad session. During these sessions, you'll hear the fiddle, Irish bagpipes, various flutes and the Irish bodhran. The sessions are based on

The Irish passion of horse racing

traditional music pieces (e.g. Jig and Reel). The songs are tied together and repeated. Almost better than these organised performances are the spontaneous social visits called cèilidh. The pubs Matt Molloy's in Westport and Furey's in Sligo are known for such gatherings.

FOOD & DRINK

Filling and savoury. To warm themselves up on cold days, the Irish love having hot meals with meat and potatoes. Homecooking is also still common. Nowadays, people look for top quality, great taste and healthy products from local manufacturers.

The Irish have really been accomplishing a lot. The *Slow Food movement* promoting enjoyable, conscious and regional food has arrived in Ireland too. Its most prominent representative is *Darina Allen*, who is very well known in Ireland. The famous TV chef and author of over a dozen cookery books is one of the pioneers of a new Irish cuisine. At her *Ballymaloe Cookery School* in Shanagarry, she shares her enjoyment of all things food-related and shows how Irish classics may be refined using only the best homemade produce. Even humble porridge can turn into a culinary epiphany at the breakfast table when the oatmeal is prepared with freshly ground grains and fresh cream.

The humble *potato*, for centuries part of the day-to-day Irish diet, offers an endless range of variations in the ways it can be prepared. There is also a large selection of *fish and seafood specialities*. Oysters (relatively inexpensive in Ireland), lobster, mussels, shrimp, as well as all kinds of fish (amongst them specialities such as shark, tuna and sea bass) appear on the menus. There is also a great variety of *speciality cheeses*. The old art of cheesemaking has been rediscovered. Some of the best farmhouse

Much more than just Irish stew and Guinness: try the many kinds of fish and crustaceans from Ireland's lakes and rivers

cheeses include *Gubbeen,* a semi-hard cow's-milk cheese, and *Gigginstown,* a raw-milk cheese. *Irish goat,* a brie-like goat's cheese, has nothing to fear from its Mediterranean rivals. Other recommended varieties are *Cashel blue* and *Burren gold* as well as *Gabriel* (traditional mountain cheese similar to Gruyère) and *Desmond,* of a softer texture. *Cais nan deise* is a hard cheese with a nutty flavour.

Prices for restaurant meals are fairly high, often only starting at 15 euros. One saving grace for those on a budget are **tourist menus**, consisting of three courses at a fixed price *(15–20 euros).* You can recognise restaurants offering this kind of menu by a small green sign showing a face with a chef's hat with *special value, tourist menu written on it.* What you get is Irish and international fare of middling quality. The higher-end restaurants will usually place you in the lounge or at the bar first to have a pre-dinner drink, before showing you to the table. Hotel gastronomy knows no days of rest, and

LOCAL SPECIALITIES

Boxty – potato pancakes
Carrageen – Atlantic seaweed used in a number of dishes
Cider – a sparkling apple wine with a low alcohol content
Coddle – a traditional stew of potatoes, sausage, onions and bacon
Crubeen – pig's trotters that are well-seasoned, smoked and salted
Fish & chips – battered and fried fish fillet served with potatoes or chips (photo right)
Fried woodcock – game bird wrapped in a slice of bacon
Irish coffee – strong hot coffee with brown sugar, a slug of whiskey and a whipped-cream top (photo left)
Irish stew – the national dish; potatoes, white cabbage, lamb and usually carrots
Kippers – grilled herrings served with a *Full Irish Breakfast*

Lamb with mint sauce – lamb served with a sour mint sauce
Porridge – a warm oat-based cereal prepared with cream or milk and served at breakfast
Scones – a small quick bread made from cake dough, served at teatime with butter, marmalade, honey and clotted cream
Seafood – anything from oysters, prawns, lobster, salmon and monkfish
Shepherd's pie – meat pie topped with mashed potatoes
Smoked Irish salmon – wild smoked salmon, usually a light pink colour and fatter than most salmon; expensive
Spring water – refreshing drinking water made and bottled in Ireland
Stout – a dark beer (Guinness being the most famous brand)
Rashers – grilled bacon served with a *Full Irish Breakfast*

in season (June to September) restaurants too will usually be open all days of the week, if often only for dinner. Alongside restaurants, cafés and pubs also offer small **snacks** or *pub grub,* like salads, sandwiches or soups. Fast-food outlets are popping up everywhere in larger towns and, for the Irish, are a welcome alternative to the fish & chip shops. For information on special restaurants and events see *www.fabulousfoodtrails.ie.* The full Irish **breakfast** is as substantial as the British one: tea or coffee with orange juice, porridge (oatmeal) and cereals, eggs and sausages, as well as bacon. All this comes with *soda bread* or *brown bread* and toast. During **lunch hour**, the Irish will often only take a light snack, with much of the working population heading for the nearest pub for a soup or sandwich. Eateries in the town centres are usually full at this time. The **main meal** is taken in the evening. *High tea* is a tradition gradually being forgotten, a meal served between 5pm and 7pm consisting of tea or coffee, bread, eggs, bacon and ham, perhaps even a small steak as well as cake.

The Irish are a nation of tea drinkers and enjoy their cuppa with fresh milk and sugar. Two well-known tea companies and expert blenders are Barry (Cork) and Bewley (Dublin).

Just as in Britain, the **pub** in Ireland is a lot more than a watering hole. The public house is a meeting place to chat and to make music, to gossip about politics, make your opinions heard and listen to others. People from all social sectors and all age groups meet at the pub, formerly (in the countryside today still) mainly men. Pubs in Ireland are split in two: the lounge, where ladies sit with their husbands or chat with a female friend, and the bar proper where drinks are pulled and served. Again as in Britain, you order your drinks at the bar and pay straight away. Pubs are usually open between 10am and midnight, on Sundays between 4pm and 11pm. Technically, young people under 18 are not allowed in, children are not well seen either, and the minimum age for occupying a seat at the bar is 21. Pubs and restaurants are subject to a smoking ban that is well observed.

While Guinness might be known as the Irish **beer**, all it is a brand name for dark

porter beer (stout); other popular brands are Beamish and Murphy's. If you order a stout, or any beer really, you will be given a pint. If you find this too much, order half a pint or simply a glass. The range of beers is similar to the UK oth-

Many meet up in the pubs in Kenmare

erwise: bitters, light lagers and ales. Last not least, Irish **whiskey** – spelt with an 'e' – is distilled three times as opposed to twice (as in the case of most Scotch whiskies), which gives it a smoother texture. The Bushmills distillery has a good range of vintage malts. Other famous brands are Jameson's, Tullamore Dew and Paddy's. Peated whiskey, while not made in Connemara, is available under the Connemara brand name.

SHOPPING

If you're looking for large department stores, you'll only find them in Dublin, Galway, Cork and Limerick. But you'll still have a great time at the small shops, and the products here are much more interesting anyway. Some of these specialise, for example, in jewellery designed with ancient Celtic motifs. You'll also come across things like film posters and handmade soaps. You'll also find plenty of stores selling everything the rural population needs to survive, like tobacco, fishing twine or the daily newspaper. Other places worth visiting are the *tea shops* and *coffee shops,* which also serve as bookshops, galleries and exhibition spaces. As far as the opening hours go, most shops open up between 9am and 9.30am and close between 5.30pm and 6pm. On Sundays, however, only a few supermarkets open their doors.

CERAMICS & JEWELLERY

Art shops and art galleries offer a large selection of pictures and ceramics, crystalware, printed fabrics and jewellery. The centuries-old Claddagh design (two hands holding a crowned heart) is used on rings and earrings today. You'll also find replicas of old Celtic fibulas.

CULINARY SOUVENIRS

A great souvenir that's easy to take with you in your carry-on bag is wild smoked salmon; a rare delicacy. It contains less fat than farmed salmon, which often owes its red colour to chemical food additives. Another option before flying back is to stock up on farmhouse cheeses made with raw milk at Dublin airport.

FASHION & DESIGN

Aran sweaters have been knitted in Ireland for a very long time, with the individual pattern symbolising the life of the Irish as fishermen. Traditionally the jumpers are made from undyed, cream-coloured wool. Real Aran jumpers will set you back around 100 euros and have the name of the woman who knitted it sewn inside.

Handwoven tweedwear comes from County Donegal and enjoys a good reputation worldwide. There is a large selection of tweed jackets in muted earthy colours, in a classic cut, and visually appealing with their leather patches and leather buttons. While the tweed might appear quite rigid to start with, it moulds itself to the wearer over

Aran sweaters and tweed jackets: knitwear and woven items are amongst the most popular souvenirs

time and becomes more rather than less beautiful as the years go by. Magee and Harris are among the better-known brands. Horse riders, fishermen, hunters and golfers will also find plenty to please them in Ireland's shops; they stock a large selection of special gear and accessories.

If you're after trendy fashion and individual design, look no further than the products of the Irish family business *Avoca (www.avoca.ie)*. The range is huge: colourful ceramics, wooden and tin toys, tweed jackets in modern fashionable designs, designer clothes for women, unusual household goods and aromatic candles, as well as unmistakable cookery books, jewellery and handmade soaps, jams, chutneys and other foodstuffs. *Avoca* products are sold in high-quality shops, as well as in their own outlets (e.g. in Powerscourt House and Moll's Gap on the Ring of Kerry). The company's headquarters are the Kilmacanogue Store

in Bray, County Wicklow, housed in the building once occupied by the Jameson whiskey company.

LACE & LINEN

Irish lace, made into tablecloths and handkerchiefs for instance, used to be a traditional industry in Limerick and Carrickmacross. Irish linen is known nationally for its quality and good value; you'll find it as tea towels and bed linen.

SPIRITS

One of the most popular spirits is whiskey: Paddy's and Jameson, as well, Bushmills in the North, distilled in the world's oldest distillery. Look out for the 10 or 12-year-old malts! The famous Baileys (Original Irish Cream), a liqueur (17 per cent) blended from Irish whiskey and cream, is another popular souvenir. Enjoy it as it is, with ice as a cocktail, or in coffee instead of milk or cream.

IN AND AROUND DUBLIN

Dublin and the Wicklow Mountains: Two sides of Ireland that couldn't be more diverse. An old capital remains forever young while County Wicklow boasts a harsh, yet beautiful landscape. Together, these two magnets pull in visitors to East Ireland both near and far.

More than a million people live in and around Dublin – nearly a quarter of the country's entire population! Life in the alleys and on the streets along the River Liffey is as lively as its young population. Everything you need to know about Dublin is in the 'Dublin' MARCO POLO travel guide.

From Dublin, a bus can take you to the Wicklow Mountains where you can hike through hilly landscapes and down deep gorges. There are nature parks, old monasteries and the 5000-year-old burial mound of Newgrange. Not only is the nature beautiful, but it's also a mystical place to experience.

DUBLIN

MAP INSIDE THE BACK COVER
(135 E4) (*M K11*) A city is changing its image: restored façades, freshly painted entrance gates, mirrored window fronts and top-range designers – Dublin has undergone revitalisation on a grand scale.

On chic Grafton Street, the scene is still dominated by buskers, students reciting poems, newspaper sellers and school kids collecting for good causes. And in

Discover the austere beauty of East Ireland! Its vibrant Irish capital is surrounded by river valleys, woods and hills

CITY **WHERE TO START?**
(U B3–4) (𝄞 b3–4)
Temple Bar: central quarter on the southern bank of the Liffey. From here, Trinity College, the Halfpenny Bridge leading across the river, the main shopping drag Grafton Street and the National Gallery are accessible on foot. Parking: Fleet Street Car Park, access via Westmoreland Street.

the evening, young and old meet up in one of the city's countless pubs to listen to music and chat away until 'last orders'. Today, traces of the Vikings' presence (the first settlers on the River Liffey) can still be found in the crypt of St Audoen's Church. These are mere ruins, however, hardly recognisable as former foundations. It took the Irish until 988 to conquer the Norse settlement, and then they had to hand it over again in 1170 to the victorious Normans. Parts of the Normans' massive city wall are still visible today.

Dublin Castle: Ancient walls and the tower of former Viking defences

The contemporary urban landscape dates back to the 18th century when entire rows of streets were erected in *Georgian style*, of which *Merrion Square* is an excellent example. And no, you aren't dreaming – those really are the terraced houses with the typical, colourful doors you've perhaps seen on postcards. And who's there relaxing on a rock, having a drink and looking up at his parents' place (no. 1)? This author only wrote a single novel, and some may know him for his fairy tales. You guessed it! Oscar Wilde. Once you've arrived at the airport, go ahead and get yourself the Dublin Pass (www.dublinpass.com). It's well worth it. It's good for one or even several days (from 49 euros up). Along with a bus transfer, it gives you free entry into 25 city attractions. The 'Dublin Freedom Pass' includes travel from the airport into the city via the Airlink Bus, a hop-on hop-off city bus tour and 3 days (72 hrs) of free travel on all Dublin buses. Pick yours up for 33 euros at the Dublin Tourism Centre or at the airport's Airlink ticket machine.

SIGHTSEEING

GUIDES & TOURS

Get your *Dublin Discovery Trails* brochures at the Dublin Tourism Centre on Suffolk Street. It explains how you can best discover the city's sights on foot. With the hop-on hop-off *Dublin Bus Tour (17.60 euros for 2 days | Wed/Fri/Sat | 59 Upper O'Connell Street | tel. 01 7 03 30 28 | www.dublinsightseeing. ie),* you can take city tours to 33 top attractions.

Guided walks to the beauty spots and hidden treasures of the city are available from INSIDER TIP *Pat Liddy's Walking Tours (from 10 euros | www.walking tours.ie)*. For a pretty view of the city from the river, take one of the *Dublin Discovered Boat Tours (leaving from*

Bachelors Walk and from 10.30am on-wards | 45 min for 15 euros | tel. 01 4 73 00 00 | www.dublindiscovered.ie). Discover Dublin by wheels with *Dublin by Bike (March–Nov daily 10am, from May also Sat/Sun 2pm | 27 euros incl. bike and helmet | www.dublincity biketours.com).* The tour (2.5 hrs) starts at *Isaacs Hostel (2–5 Frenchman's Lane | near Busaras)* and takes you to the main sight.

DUBLIN CASTLE (U A–B4) *(ⅲ a–b4)*

Is this a palace or a castle? After the 70-minute tour through the structure, you'll see it's both. This 700-year-old fortress has been rebuilt and built upon time and time again. It's highlights are the lavishly furnished State Apartments and St Patrick's Hall where Queen Elizabeth and Barack Obama were once guests and even Irish presidents were inaugurated. Make sure to see 'The Medieval Undercroft' in the excavation site of old Viking defences. Part of the River Poddle flows underground here, as well. *Mon–Sat 10am–5pm, Sun 12pm–5pm | admission 7 euros, tour 10 euros | Dame Street | www.dublincastle.ie*

DUBLIN WRITERS MUSEUM ● (U B2) *(ⅲ b2)*

A homage to Ireland's poets and authors. By entering this Georgian, architectural masterpiece, you'll be thrown into the world of four Nobel Prize winners and of other poets. You'll see the first editions of their works, James Joyce's waistcoat, and Samuel Beckett's glasses. Next door is the Irish Writers' Centre where you can speak with future authors personally. *Mon–Sat 10am–5pm, Sun 11am–5pm | admission 7.50 euros | 18 Parnell Square | www.writersmuseum.com*

GUINNESS STOREHOUSE (0) *(ⅲ 0)*

Here, in Europe's largest brewery, is where Guinness has been brewing for over 200 years. After taking your tour through the *Guinness Storehouse,* a spectacularly renovated warehouse, you'll be served a cold pint of – what else!? – Guinness (included in admission). Get your pint at the ⚸ *Gravity Bar* on the 7th floor. *Daily 9.30am–7pm, July/Aug till 8pm | admission 20 euros | St James' Gate | Crane Street | www.guinness-storehouse. com | Bus 13, 40, 123 from D'Olier Street | Bus 40 from O'Connell Street*

⭐ **National Gallery of Ireland**
A must for art lovers, who will find numerous masterpieces of European painting → p. 36

⭐ **Temple Bar**
Hipsters will enjoy this: in Dublin's most popular quarter, the art and pub scene rub shoulders → p. 38

⭐ **Old Library**
Order a copy of any book that was ever printed in Great Britain into the reading room → p. 39

⭐ **Monasterboice**
5th-century monastic ruins with tall High Crosses of unique beauty → p. 44

⭐ **Newgrange**
At winter solstice, the sun's rays shine into the inner chamber of this prehistoric passage tomb → p. 44

⭐ **Powerscourt Gardens**
Tea and scones on the terrace of Powerscourt House, with a superb view of one of the most beautiful landscape gardens in Ireland → p. 45

MARCO POLO HIGHLIGHTS

HALFPENNY BRIDGE ⚓
(U B3) (🗺 b3)

This small pedestrian bridge appears in most Dublin holiday shots. For centuries, boats and ferries took Dubliners across the Liffey. In the 19th century, life became easier when a metal bridge over the river was financed with a half-penny toll per crossing. Today it's free. *City centre west of O'Connell Bridge*

JAMES JOYCE CENTRE (U B2) (🗺 b2)

A day of remembrance for a novel's fictional hero? Although it's not an official holiday, it doesn't stop the Irish from celebrating *Bloomsday* (see p. 116) to honour Leopold Bloom. Well, actually they're honouring James Joyce who gave this name to the advertising agent he though up in his novel 'Ulysses'. But what's this James Joyce myth going around? You'll find out here! After the tour, do like Bloom would and treat yourself to a gorgonzola sandwich and a glass of Burgundy in the nearby pub *Dave Byrnes (21 Duke Street). Mon–Sat 10am–5pm, Sun 12pm–5pm | admission 5 euros | 35 North Great George's Street | www.jamesjoyce.ie*

KILMAINHAM GAOL (O) (🗺 O)

It's Easter 1916. The Irish Republican Brotherhood launch an Easter Rebellion against the occupying British troops. The uprising fails and the leaders are thrown into the prison Kilmainham Gaol. Dark halls, musty cells and dungeons. Later, 14 rebels are executed on site in this dreary-looking courtyard. Non only the sensitive kind get the creeps when visiting this prison. First built in 1796, the prison has been closed for almost a year now. This shocking tour is always a good lesson in Irish history. *April–Sept daily 9.30am–6pm, Oct–March Mon–Sat 9.30pm–6pm | admission 7 euros (in-*cludes tour) | Inchicore Road | Dublin | Kilmainham | www.heritageireland.ie | Bus 69 from Aston Quay*

LIFFEY BOARD WALK (U B3) (🗺 b3)

A wooden boardwalk leading along the Liffey's northern bank from O'Connell Bridge to Halfpenny Bridge, ideal for a leisurely stroll. Part of the riverbank (at Lower Ormond Quay) was converted into an *Italian Quarter* (also known as Quartier Bloom) with Italian restaurants and shops.

NATIONAL GALLERY OF IRELAND ★ ●
(U C4) (🗺 c4)

An oasis of calm and a journey into the world of high art: works by Jack B. Yeats, Ireland's most important 20th-century artist, as well as a Caravaggio discovered in Dublin are amongst the gems of this collection of European art. Workshops and free guided tours by art students, concerts and special exhibitions. *Mon–Sat 9.30am–5.30pm, Thu 9.30am–8.30pm, Sun noon–5.30pm | free admission | Merrion Square West | next to Leinster House | www.nationalgallery.ie*

OLD JAMESON DISTILLERY
(U A3) (🗺 a3)

Since the worldwide successful whiskey brand moved production to Midleton (near Cork), the distillery, built in 1780, only houses a show distillery. Still, on a guided tour you will hear how the 'water of life' is produced. *Daily 9.30am–6pm | distillery tour including a drink 14 euros | Bow Street | Smithfield Village | www.jamesonwhiskey.com*

ROYAL HOSPITAL KILMAINHAM ●
(O) (🗺 O)

Built in the 17th century as a military pensioners' home, the building today serves as a *National Centre for Cul-*

The National Gallery: A European art exhibition featuring Caravaggio and many others

ture and the Arts with exhibitions, concerts, theatre and cultural events of all kinds. It also houses the excellent *IMMA*, the *Irish Museum of Modern Art (www. imma.ie). Tue–Sat 11.30am–5.30pm, Sun noon–5.30 pm | free admission | Military Road | Kilmainham | www.rhk. ie | buses 26, 51, 51B, 78A, 79, 90, 123*

INSIDER TIP SKYLINE CROKE PARK
(0) (*ĿLJ K11*)

600 m/656 yd-long, this walkway circles the rooftop of the Croke Park Stadium. You'll take over 100 steps to reach a height of 44 m/144 ft above the ground. From the walkway's five platforms, you'll have a view over all of Dublin. *Tours (2 hrs): daily from 10.30am, depending on the season; tour times monthly on the website | tour 20 euros | start: GAA Museum, east side of Croke Park Stadium,* *Clonliffe Road, off St Joseph's Av. | www. crokepark.ie | Busses 3, 11, 11a, 16, 16a, 41*

INSIDER TIP SMITHFIELD VILLAGE
(U A3) (*ĿLJ a3*)

The restored block north of the Liffey is following the path of Temple Bar to become a hip district, too. Here, along with several arts institutions, you'll find many restaurants, bars, a hotel, and the *Old Jameson Distillery* (1780), which is now a museum. *Between Bow and Smithfield Street, west of O'Connell Street*

ST PATRICK'S CATHEDRAL
(U A5) (*ĿLJ a5*)

A bulwark of faith for 1500 years, this is the place where the 'Apostle of Ireland' St Patrick baptised his followers. Ireland's largest cathedral was erected in 1193. Inside, you'll find where Jonathan Swift, the writer of 'Gulliver's Travels' is buried. Not only did he have a great imagination, he was also a dean at St Patrick's from 1713 to 1745. *Mon–Fri 9am–5pm, Sat 9am–6pm, Sun 9–10.30am, 12.30–3pm, 4.30–6pm | admission 6 euros | St Patrick's Close | www.stpatrickscathe dral.ie*

SWENY'S PHARMACY ● (0) *(ᗝ 0)*

A must-see for fans of 'Ulysses', the classic novel by James Joyce. Here in this former pharmacy (1853) is where the novel's protagonist, Leopold Bloom bought his lemon soap. The house is now maintained by Joyce fans offering second-hand books, the literature journal 'Joyce Quarterly' and Joyce readings with free admission. *Mon–Sat 11am–5pm, readings Mon–Fri 1pm, Thu 1 and 7pm, Sat 11am | admission free | 1 Lincoln Place | Dublin | www.swenys.ie*

TEMPLE BAR ★ (U B3–4) *(ᗝ b3–4)*

Experience street art and rock music in Dublin's hip quarter. Browse alternative, long-established shops and vintage boutiques. Enjoy French haute cuisine or discover the local restaurant scene.

The Temple Bar's cultural exchange is its highlight. The *Projects Arts Centre* is based here. Exciting events and exhibitions take place on stage with the *Irish Film Centre* (showing classic films and small Irish productions), the *Gallery of Photography* (photo exhibitions and workshops) and the *Temple Bar Gallery* (where many artists show their work). Get a detailed map and a sightseeing pass (includes discounts and a list of members) at the *Temple Bar Cultural*

The Old Library: The Reading Room holds hundreds of thousands of precious books

Trust. *(12 East Essex Street | tel. 01 6 77 22 55). Between Westmoreland and Fishamble Street, southeast of Halfpenny Bridge*

TRINITY COLLEGE LIBRARY (U C4) (*m c4*)

Founded in 1592, Ireland's oldest and most renowned university is situated right at the heart of the city centre and charms visitors with its splendid Georgian buildings and landscaped park. Built between 1712 and 1732, the ★ *Old Library* is incredible. In the *Long Room,* a 70 m/ 230 ft-long room with a wooden vaulted roof, shutters protect the 200,000 oldest of the 4.5 million books in the College's collection from the sun. The exhibits include a rare copy of the Easter proclamation of the Irish Republic of 1916. The *Book of Kells* is true gem. This illuminated manuscript is an early Christian masterpiece made up of 680 pages of Latin text. It artistically presents the four Gospels in fine detail and boasts Celtic paintings. Every day they turn a page, so you never know what pages you'll see displayed! *May–Sept Mon–Sat 8.30am–5pm, Sun 9.30am–5pm, Oct–April Mon–Sat 9.30am–5pm, Sun 12pm–4.30pm | admission 11 euros | between Nassau and Pearse Street, entrance in College Street | www.tcd.ie/library*

FOOD & DRINK

A 2.5-hour guided tour of markets and shops with tastings, *Dublin Tasting Trail (Fri/Sat 10am–12.30pm | tel. 01 4 97 12 45 | 55 euros | www.fabfoodtrails.ie)* is always an excellent stand-in for lunch.

BEWLEY'S CAFE (U B4) (*m b4*)

This is THE meet-up place in Dublin! Since 1927, they've been serving coffee, tea, pasta and salads in a young modern environment. *Mon–Wed 8am–10pm, Thu–Sat 8am–11pm, Sun 9am–10pm | 78/79 Grafton Street | tel. 01 6 72 77 20 | www.bewleys.com | Budget*

CHAPTER ONE (U B2) (*m b2*)

Head chef Ross Lewis' creations, beautifully fusing haute cuisine and rustic Irish fare, earned him a Michelin Star. Two affordable options are the *Set Lunch* (32.50 euros) and the *Pre Theatre Menu* (39.50 euros) which can be ordered up until 6pm. *Tue–Fri 12.30–2pm, Tue–Sat 5.30–10pm | 18–19 Parnell Square | tel. 01 8 73 22 66 | www.chapteronerestaurant.com | Expensive*

COPPINGER ROW (U B4) (*m b4*)

A young scene with fresh, Mediterranean cuisine. Moroccan lentil soup with chickpeas and lamb, tuna with aubergine; in good weather also outside seating. *Daily 12pm–11pm | 48 Coppinger Row | from South William Street | tel. 01 6 72 98 84 | www.coppingerrow.com | Moderate–Expensive*

CORNUCOPIA (U B4) (*m b4*)

The location hasn't changed in 30 years. The vegan and vegetarian dishes Deirdre serves here are delicious, creative and made with regional ingredients. Her recipes have even been published in a cookery book called 'Cornucopia at Home'. Go ahead and pick it up after your meal! *Mon–Sat 8.30am–10pm, Sun noon–10pm | 19 Wicklow Street | tel. 01 6 77 75 83 | www.cornucopia.ie | Moderate*

GOVINDA'S (U B3) (*m b3*)

Delicious vegetarian dishes: eat well and cheap in the spiritually inspired Kirtan Centre (yoga and meditation available too) in the centre of Dublin. *Mon–Sat noon–9pm, Sun noon–7pm | 83 Middle Abbey Street | tel. 01 4 75 03 09 | www.govindas.ie | Budget*

THE MARKET BAR
(U B4) *(ℳ b4)*

Cheap and chic. Cooked garlic hovers over the large, shaded patio, as well as the warehouse of a historical red brick building. Tapas, salads, and delightful soups served in an attractively styled loft environment. A great place to take a

a glass-roofed inner courtyard, as well as the *Westbury Shopping Mall,* both located near Grafton Street.

BROWN THOMAS (U B4) *(ℳ b4)*
Founded in 1849, this department store stocks everything that's fancy, expensive and currently hip: from Hunter wel-

Grafton Street: Top address for shopping queens!

long break. *Sun–Thu noon–11.30pm, Fri/Sat 1.30pm–1.30am | 14a Fade Street | tel. 01 6 13 90 94 | www.marketbar.ie | Moderate–Expensive*

SHOPPING

Dublin's main shopping drags are Grafton Street and the cheaper O'Connell Street and Henry Street. Dodge any rain showers with a stroll through the indoor shopping malls at St Stephen's Green. Also pleasant: the ● *Powerscourt Centre*: boutiques and cafés stretching along

lies via Stella McCartney's design creations to perfume by Jo Malone. Look out for the sales in January and July, when items are reduced up to 60 per cent. *88–95 Grafton Street | www.browntho mas.com*

FALLON & BYRNE (U B4) *(ℳ b4)*
Trendy gourmet trio across three storeys: market-fresh groceries are sold in the food hall in light, contemporary design, there is an ⊕ organic restaurant and a large wine cellar. *11–17 Exchequer Street | www.fallonandbyrne.com*

KILKENNY SHOP (U C4) (𝒲 c4)

The go-to place for everything typical Irish! Ceramics in earthy colours, waxed raincoats, tweed scarves and jackets, cashmere and lambswool jumpers, linen, lace and woodcarvings. They aren't cheap but of the highest quality. *6–15 Nassau Street | www.kilkennyshop.com*

INSIDER TIP MOORE STREET MARKET (U B3) (𝒲 b3)

This market is a reminder of how Dublin once was. Buy fruit, vegetables and flowers at the street stands. Some of the products are even delivered by horse and cart. *Mon–Sat 9am–1pm | Moore Street*

INSIDER TIP RORY'S FISHING TACKLE (U B3) (𝒲 b3)

An institution for over 50 years! Rory, a friendly owner and fisherman, has everything anglers need, from live bait to willow baskets. *17a Temple Bar | www. rorys.ie*

ENTERTAINMENT

ABBEY THEATRE (U C3) (𝒲 c3)

Today's national theatre, founded in 1904 by William Butler Yeats, regularly showcases Irish authors. An entertaining and affordable (tickets from 10 euros) night out in a lovely, old-fashioned part of the city, guaranteed! *26 Lower Abbey Street | tel. 01 8 78 72 22 | www. abbeytheatre.ie*

BUTTON FACTORY (U B3) (𝒲 b3)

Rock, underground, crossover – daily live music from newcomers and Irish stars. *Curved Street | tel. 01 6 70 91 05 | www. buttonfactory.ie*

THE BRAZEN HEAD (U A4) (𝒲 a4)

The city's oldest pub – established since 1198! ● Live music daily, and the rooms fill up early. In summer, people sit in the courtyard, and in winter it's a meeting place for smokers. *20 Lower Bridge Street | www.brazenhead.com*

DUBLIN LITERARY PUB CRAWL ● (U B4) (𝒲 b4)

Drink Guinness and listen to poetry as two actors entertain and lead you into various pubs – places which were once a hub of inspiration for famous Irish poets and thinkers. The meeting point is at *The Duke (9 Duke Street | April– Oct daily 7.30pm, Nov–March Thu–Sun 7.30pm | 13 euros). www.dublinpub crawl.com*

INSIDER TIP THE MEZZ (U B4) (𝒲 b4)

House, techno, funk & soul live on stage! The music is always loud, lively and full of attitude! *Daily | admission usually free | 23/24 Eustace Street | tel. 01 6 70 76 55 | www.mezz.ie*

MOTHER (U B4) (𝒲 b4)

Dublin's top DJs perform electro, house, and even the disco hits of the 70s here! A gay club and popular weekend hang out that even heterosexuals enjoy. 21 to enter! *Sat 11pm–3.30am | admission 10 euros | 23 Eustace Street | www.mother club.ie*

MUSICAL PUB CRAWL ● (U B3) (𝒲 b3)

Fancy listening to some pipes, fiddle and the accordion? At this two-and-a-half-hour pub crawl, two musicians lead you through the vibrant pubs of the Temple Bar quarter. Along the way, they play some music and tell the history of Irish music. *Starts April–Oct daily 7.30pm, Nov–March Tue–Sat 7.30pm at Oliver Street, John Gogarty's pub | 2 euros | Anglesea Street | tel. 01 4 75 33 13 | www. discoverdublin.ie/musical-pub-crawl*

O'DONOGHUE'S (U C5) (*m c5*)

The cradle that rocked The Dubliners! The walls display Impressive pictures and it's always jam-packed! No doubt a classic pub! *15 Merrion Row | tel. 01 6 60 71 94 | www.odonoghues.ie*

PROJECT ARTS CENTRE (U B3) (*m b 3*)

Rock concerts, avant-garde productions, modern dance and art exhibitions are put on at this arts centre in the popular Temple Bar. *39 East Essex Street | tel. 01 8 81 96 13 | www.projectartscentre.ie*

THE STAG'S HEAD (U B4) (*m b4*)

One of the most beautiful Victorian pubs and they've been stocked with Bulmers Cider and Smithwick's Ale since 1770. *Mon–Sat 10.30am–1am, Sun till midnight | 1 Dame Court | tel. 01 6 79 37 01*

LOW BUDGET

The *An Oige Hostel* (*364 beds | 61 Mountjoy Street | tel. 01 8 30 17 66 | www.anoige.ie | buses 16, 46A, 16A*) is a cheap alternative to a hotel.

Second-hand wares and markets; every weekend in the Temple Bar quarter: *Cow's Lane Designer Market* (Sat | Cow's Lane), *Temple Bar Food Market* (Sat | Meeting House Square), *Temple Bar Book Market, Temple Bar Square* (Sat/Sun 11am–6pm | Temple Bar Square)

The *Rambler Ticket* for Dublin's buses (including the bus from and to the airport) is particularly good value. For 5 days you pay 31.50 euros. They are sold at the airport and in many shops.

THE TEMPLE BAR (U B3) (*m b3*)

Every evening, you can enjoy ● live Irish folk music in this popular pub – free of charge! *47/48 Temple Bar | tel. 01 6 72 52 86 | www.thetemplebarpub. com*

WHERE TO STAY

INSIDER TIP ▶ **ARLINGTON HOTEL** (U B3) (*m b3*)

Located beautifully on the banks of the Liffey and on O'Connell Bridge, this Georgian hotel often offers affordable accommodation. Folk music and shows on a daily basis in a medieval-themed bar. Also popular with Americans following in the footsteps of their ancestors. *131 rooms | 23/25 Bachelors Walk | tel. 01 8 04 91 00 | www.arlington.ie | Moderate*

AVALON HOUSE (U B5) (*m b5*)

A Victorian guesthouse with a central location and plenty of dorms, single and double rooms. Communal spaces are also available. Wi-Fi and bike rentals. Free Continental breakfast. Café/restaurant. *71 rooms with 281 beds | 55 Aungier Street | tel. 01 4 75 00 01 | www.avalonhouse.ie | Budget*

THE CASTLE HOTEL (U B2) (*m b2*)

This friendly, comfortably furnished hotel stretches over several Georgian townhouses. The *Castle Vaults Bar* has Guinness on tap and (at weekends) live music. Even the (Irish) guests sing along at times. *131 rooms | 2–4 Gardiner Row/ Great Denmark Street | tel. 01 8 74 69 49 | www.castle-hotel.ie | Moderate*

THE CLARENCE (U B4) (*m b4*)

After investing 2 million euros to buy this historical two-star hotel on the River Liffey, Bono and 'The Edge' of U2 have

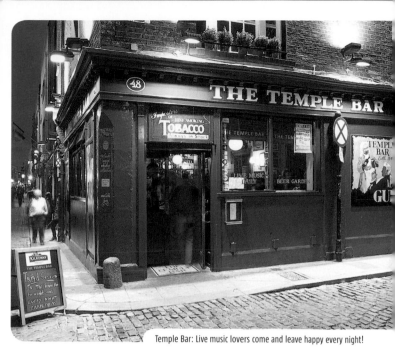

Temple Bar: Live music lovers come and leave happy every night!

proven themselves to be people of fine taste. The hotel is now one of Dublin's top locations. Furnished with Shaker furniture, the hotel's simple design is practical. In the hotel's *Octagon Bar*, you might run into the band members if they're back home visiting. Either way, the cocktails always taste great! *44 rooms | 6–8 Wellington Quay | tel. 01 4 07 08 00 | www.theclarence.ie | Expensive*

INFORMATION

DUBLIN TOURISM CENTRE
(U B4) *(ⓜ b4)*
St Andrew's Church | 25 Suffolk Street | tel. 1850 23 03 30 (*) | www.visitdublin. com Additional offices at the airport, in Dún Laoghaire port, at 14 O'Connell Street and Baggot Street Bridge

WHERE TO GO

DÚN LAOGHAIRE (135 E4) *(ⓜ K11)*
The fast DART suburban train brings you to the port town (pop. 60,000) just under 11 km/7 mi south of the city. There are great views of Dublin Bay from here, especially on a stroll along the eastern ☀ harbour walls. Catch a glimpse of Celtic symbols in the *oratory* at the Dominican convent *(Lower George's Street)*.

GLENDALOUGH ☀ **(135 E5)** *(ⓜ J12)*
Only 48 km/30 mi south of Dublin, a unique hiking and natural paradise awaits you: numerous routes taking several days, between 60 and 100 km/37 and 62 mi, lead through the hilly country of the *Wicklow Mountains*. Amongst the

highlights of this area, the narrow valley of Glendalough encompasses two green shimmering lakes, framed by mountains. Founded in the 7th century by Saint Kevin, the ● monastery of the same name *(admission visitor centre 5 euros | www.glendalough.ie)* soon became the spiritual centre of Ireland. From the 9th century onwards, the round tower, 33 m/108 ft high, a refuge for the monks during Viking attacks, stood at the heart of the monastic town. Nature lovers should take the *Falcon Trail*, a 4-km/2.5-mi hiking trail, at the Upper Lake.

KILDARE (134 C5) (*Ⓜ H12*)

The town (pop. 4200) featuring 18th-century houses lies 48 km/30 mi west of Dublin (on the N 7) in the heart of the Irish horse country. You absolutely have to visit the famous *Irish National Stud (daily 9am–6pm | 12.50 euros | Tully | Brallistown Little | www.irishnationalstud.ie)* in Tully, 2 km/1.2 mi to the east. After seeing Ireland's legendary thoroughbred horses and visiting the Horse Museum, stroll through the Japanese garden (boasting a lovely restaurant) and appreciate the 200-year-old bonsai trees. Visitors also enjoy shopping at *Kildare Village (Mon–Wed 10am–7pm Thu–Sun till 8pm | Nurney Road | www.kildarevillage.com)*, an outlet shopping centre with a Disney-like design. Here you can buy designer clothing (e.g. Ralph Lauren, Mulberry, etc.) and enjoy one of their cafés or restaurants.

KILLINEY (135 E4) (*Ⓜ K12*)

Bono, Van Morrison and even Enya all live in the two seaside resorts of Killiney and Dalkey (southeast 12 km/7.5 mi). This place is filled with stars, bankers and top managers. The sights here are simply fantastic. Why? Well, come and see for yourself! Take a stroll in the ☘

surrounding hill country, to Dalkey for instance. At the top, you'll have one of the prettiest views of Killiney Bay and Dublin.

MONASTERBOICE ★ ●
(135 E2) (*Ⓜ J10*)

The old Round Tower is over 33 m/108 ft tall and stand alone (north 56 km/34 mi) among an early Christian monastery. **INSIDER TIP** With there being so few visitors, the atmosphere is almost mystical here between October and April. Have a look at the artistically made Muiredach's Cross. One of three high crosses, this one boasts decorative stone carvings depicting Cain's murder of Abel and Adam being tempted by Eve. Can you recognise any other biblical scenes? *www.monasterboice.net*

NEWGRANGE ★ ●
(135 D2–3) (*Ⓜ J10*)

Some 5000 years old, the burial chamber 58 km/36 mi northwest of Dublin is

a wonder of early architecture. The interior of the megalithic burial mound, some 75 m/246 ft long and 13 m/43 ft high, can only be entered through a narrow passage 18 m/59 ft long. Above the entrance is an opening through which the sun reaches the burial chamber, bathing it in light on five days, around 21 December, at the winter solstice, for 15 minutes. It is said that the stones at those times appear as if dipped in gold. *In summer 9am–7pm, in winter 9am–5pm | admission by guided tour only, every half-hour | admission 7 euros | bookings at the Visitors' Centre on the L 21, 1.9 km/1.2 mi west of Donore | www.newgrange.com*

From Mon–Fri 9.50am (Sat/Sun 8am), a shuttle bus *(40 euros incl. admission | tel. 086 3 55 13 55 | www.newgrange tours.com)* leaves from Shelbourne Hotel (St Stephen's Green) to Newgrange. The return journey is at 4.30pm.

POWERSCOURT GARDENS ★ ●
(135 E5) *(🛉 K12)*

Powerscourt Gardens is one of Ireland's most beautiful parks. On the grounds is the imposing *Powerscourt Estate.* This manor house is surrounded by greenery and has a Japanese garden and pet cemetery. There's a castle park, a waterfall *(5 km/3 mi)* and an elegant café terrace with a superb natural backdrop. Next door in *Powerscourt House*, the small maze at the INSIDER TIP *Avoca Store* is a delight for anyone looking for colourful, imaginative gifts. *Daily 9.30am–5.30pm | admission 7 euros, waterfall 6 euros | Enniskerry | 18 km/11 mi south of Dublin | www.powerscourt.com | bus 44 from Dublin.* Next to Powerscourt Gardens, the *Hotel Powerscourt (200 rooms | Enniskerry | tel. 01 2 74 88 88 | www.power scourthotel.com | Expensive)* is a hotel in the Palladian style with ☼ suites boasting views of the *Sugarloaf Mountains.*

The Round Tower at Glendalough: A former refuge for monks and a peaceful landscape

THE SOUTH

Picture-postcard Ireland: if one region comes close to the cliché of an intact world with charming landscape, picturesque villages and dramatic coastline, it's the south. Turn literally any corner and a new highlight is revealed.

Cork too, the country's second-largest city, gives an impression of good spirits and wealth. Numerous fishing villages nearby look so trim and picturesque that you want to stay forever. In Beara, Iveragh and Dingle, peninsulas popular with Irish visitors too poke out into the Atlantic. Try to go around at least one of them by car – and you will fall for their beauty, guaranteed. More small islands, and very interesting ones at that – such as the Blaskets – lie off the coast. Stretching out towards the north, the undulating and

fertile hills of Co. Limerick, predominantly used for agriculture, are scattered with small towns from Norman times and picturesque river valleys.

CORK

MAP INSIDE THE BACK COVER
(138 A5) (𝄞 E16) There's a down-right pleasant air about Cork, the country's second-largest city (pop. 126,000) with its many bridges across the river Lee. You will see plenty of students of UCC (University College Cork) sitting in the street cafés in front of Georgian façades.

A number of excellent restaurants are within easy walking distance, as well

A rocky coastline and hidden coves: the southern fishing villages boast colourful houses – and all have pubs!

CITY WHERE TO START?
St Patrick's Street: branching off from this shopping street are various pedestrian zones with beautifully restored Georgian houses. St Patrick's Bridge leads across the River Lee into the northern parts of the city. The bus station and a multi-storey car park are on the other side of the river, at the eastern end of Merchant's Quay.

as many pubs and shops. Corkonians are experts in the art of the good life – and also in spending a lot of money. Just check out the long queues at the cashpoints.

The word *cork* derives from the Gaelic Corcaigh meaning *marsh* or *boggy terrain*. The city stretches out across an island amidst the River Lee, which splits into two arms here. These days, 25 bridges lead across the river and many of the roads were once waterways. Even the main shopping drag of St Patrick's

The Crawford Art Gallery: Schoolchildren contemplating the art in the morning

Street still served as moorings for cargo ships in 1750. There has been a known settlement here since the Middle Ages, with St Finbarr founding his monastic school around the year 650. However, the only building that remains from this time, Red Abbey, was outside the town. During the siege of Cork by the English the city wall was completely destroyed in 1690; some foundations are still visible near the entrance arch in Bishop Lucey Park and in the Grand Parade Hotel. With the 19th-century establishment of the butter market, today situated on Shandon Hill, trade with Spain, Holland, Germany, North America and the West Indies was given a substantial boost. Magnificent Georgian and Victorian townhouses are a reminder of the wealth of the time.

SIGHTSEEING

CORK BUTTER MUSEUM

Happy cows! At the *Butter Market,* discover how dairy farming, butter production and butter trade developed from the 19th century to Kerrygold. *March–June, Sept/Oct daily 10am–5pm, July/Aug daily 10am–6pm, Nov–Feb Sat/Sun 11am–3pm | admission 4 euros | Exchange Street | O'Connell Square | www.corkbutter. museum*

CORK CITY GAOL

Established in 1824, this palace-looking prison was used for 100 years by the British to cage mostly political inmates. Today the building houses an impressive museum. Step into tiny cells as door screeching sounds and echoing footsteps play over your headphones and learn of the fate of former inmates. *Daily April–Sept 9.30am–4pm, Oct–March 10am–4pm | admission 8 euros | Convent Av. | from Sunday's Well Road | www.cork citygaol.com*

CORK PUBLIC MUSEUM

Discover Cork's history in a charming Georgian house from early Christianity up to the early 20th-century. The documents about the revolt against the British and the exhibition on the Easter Rising in 1916 are interesting. *April–Sept Mon–Fri 11am–1pm and 2–5pm, Sat 11am–1pm and 2–4pm, Sun 3–5pm | admission free | Mardyke Walk | Fitzgerald Park*

COURT HOUSE

A mix of architectural styles. The courthouse from 1853 has an impressive front façade with Corinthian columns. The back has a Tudor style. To top it off, the interior boasts red and green marble. *Washington Street*

CRAWFORD ART GALLERY ●

Visiting the art gallery in the morning is unique – you're likely to have it to yourself! Built in 1724 as a customs house, the building now houses works by Old Masters and modern Irish artists, as well as replicas of statues from antiquity. There's an affordable café and restaurant, too. *Mon–Sat 10am–5pm, Thu until 8pm | admission free | Emmet Place | www.crawfordartgallery.ie*

FITZGERALD PARK

Lying between Western Road and the Lee (access from Mardyke Walk), the green heart of Cork boasts various entertainment options, fine sculptures, the city museum and a reasonably priced café.

GRAND PARADE

This broad street forms the backbone of the city today. It used to be a canal and is limited by the southern arm of the river

---

★ **Skellig Michael**
The summit of the 217 m/712 ft high, pyramid-shaped rock island is occupied by an Early Christian ecclesiastical complex → p. 64

★ **Cork City Market**
A piece of England on the Emerald Isle: discover impressive arches, fountains and galleries in the Victorian halls from 1876 while strolling through the organic market → p. 52

★ **Blarney Castle**
Stronghold boasting a mythical stone that even Sir Walter Scott kissed back in the day → p. 55

★ **Youghal**
Pretty harbour town with historic city wall from the 13th century → p. 58

★ **Muckross House**
Splendid Victorian manor house at the heart of a national park → p. 58

★ **Ring of Kerry**
Coastal panorama road in arguably the most beautiful part of Ireland → p. 63

★ **Kinsale**
Picture perfect: Timbered buildings, forts and fresh fish → p. 64

MARCO POLO HIGHLIGHTS

Lee, by the City Market and Bishop Lucey Park. The park has remnants of the old city wall. The entrance gate is from 1850. At its southern end, the Grand Parade is overlooked by the *National Monument*. This was erected for four rebels who fell fighting against the British (1798–1867).

RED ABBEY TOWER

The square tower forms part of a former medieval Augustinian monastery, making it the oldest building in town. *Red Abbey Street*

SHANDON CHURCH & BELLS ⚲

Visible from afar, St Anne's church atop a hill north of the river Lee was built in 1722. One peculiarity is the weathervane in the shape of a salmon, with a 3 m/10 ft span. For a fee, the famous glockenspiel can be set to work. *June–Sept Mon–Sat 10am–5pm, Sun 11.30am–4.30pm, March–May, Oct Mon–Sat 10am–4pm, Sun 11.30am–15.30pm, Nov–Feb Mon–Sat 11am–3pm, Sun 11.30am–3pm | admission 5 euros | Shandon Street www. shandonbells.ie*

ST FINBARR'S CATHEDRAL

St Finbarr is said to have founded a monastery on the site of this church around 650. Designed in the Gothic style by architect William Burgess, the church with its 40-m/131-ft tower was consecrated in 1870. Watch out for the marble work inside, the window rose in the west front and the numerous sculptures. *Mon–Sat 9.30am–5.30pm, Sun 1.30pm–2.30pm and 4.30pm–6pm | admission 5 euros | between Dean and Bishop Street | www. corkcathedral.webs.com*

ST PATRICK'S BRIDGE

After several bridges across the river Lee had been destroyed by flooding, the current bridge at the northern end of St Patrick's Street was constructed in 1861 from limestone. Boasting a perfectly worked balustrade and three beautifully curved arches, this is a true beauty of a bridge. *Bridge Street*

UNIVERSITY COLLEGE CORK

Founded in 1845, the university is Ireland's leading research institution. The campus boasts buildings in the Tudor Gothic style (the central quadrangle in particular) as well as the *Honan Chapel* and its lead windows. The Visitors' Centre *(tel. 021 4 90 18 76)* in the Stone Corridor of the North Wing is open Mon–Fri 9am–5pm and Sat noon–5pm. *Main entrance Western Road/Donovan's Road | www.ucc.ie*

FOOD & DRINK

INSIDER TIP CAFÉ PARADISO

Bistro serving top vegetarian fare. Chef Denis Cotter is considered a creative genius when it comes to green spelt and chard. In his fourth cookbook 'For the Love of Food', he reveals some of his best recipes for you to try at home. The restaurant offers a two or three-course pre-theatre dinner for 23 and 29 euros respectively from Mondays to Saturdays between 5.30pm and 6.45 pm. *Mon–Sat 5.30–10pm | 16 Lancaster Quay/Western Road | tel. 021 4 27 79 39 | www.cafepara diso.ie | Expensive*

THE FARMGATE CAFÉ

Meeting place on the gallery of the *English Food Market*. Specialities: fish and poultry, as well as Irish cheeses. *Mon–Sat 8.30am–5pm | Princes Street | tel. 021 4 27 81 34 | www.farmgate.ie | Budget*

FOUR LIARS BISTRO

Good pit-stop for a cocktail or a light dinner before hitting the town: chicken in a sauce of forest mushrooms and potato-salmon paté are among the classics served here. 10am–10pm | *Butter Exchange* | *Shandon* | *tel. 021 439 40 40* | *www.thefourliarsbistro.com* | *Moderate*

GREENES RESTAURANT

An old, 18th-century warehouse converted into a modern restaurant. The cheaper *Early Bird Menu* is available from 6pm to 7pm. *Daily noon–2pm, 5.30pm–9pm* | *48 McCurtain Street* | *tel. 021 4 55 22 79* | *www.greenes.restaurant.com* | *Moderate*

JACOBS ON THE MALL

Modern purist design in a historic building (former Turkish baths), ambitious contemporary cuisine combining Irish cooking traditions with international influences. Unpretentious for lunch, stylish and refined for dinner. One choice for afters never disappoints: butterscotch pudding. *Mon–Sat 5pm–10pm* | *30 South Mall* | *tel. 021 4 25 15 30* | *www.jacobs onthemall.com* | *Moderate*

JACQUES

This is the best place to go in town! Jacques has been committed to excellent French cooking for over 30 years. Much recommended are the two-course changing menus *(24 euros)*. It's best to make a reservation. *Mon 10am–4pm, Tue–Sat 10am–10pm* | *23 Oliver Plunkett Street* | *near the main post office* | *tel. 021 4 27 73 87* | *www.jacquesrestaurant. ie* | *Expensive*

QAY CO-OP ☺

Founded in 1982, this place is a stalwart for vegetarians and fans of organic food. In the restaurant, they offer vegetarian pizza, lasagne, soup, and salads. Their vegetables are all organic and can even be purchased to take home at the counter. In addition, they offer goods at their organic bakery and in the small grocery store. *Mon–Sat 10am–10pm* | *24 Sullivan's Quay* | *tel. 021 4 31 70 26* | *www. quaycoop.com* | *Budget*

Life on St Patrick's Street: Cork's main shopping mile

SCOOZI'S

This family-friendly restaurant serves pizzas, lasagne and other Italian classics. *Mon–Sat 8am–9pm, Sun noon–9pm | 2–5 Winthrop Lane | tel. 021 4 27 50 77 | www.scoozis.ie | Budget*

SHOPPING

COAL QUAY MARKET

Second-hand goods from hats to shoes, also fresh and new items ranging from a head of cabbage to CDs: all this is on offer in historic halls, at street stalls, in tiny shops as well as by flying vendors. *Sat 9am–5pm | Cornmarket Street*

CORK CITY MARKET ★ ⊙

With its architecture of arches, fountains and galleries, the attractive market complex built in 1786 in the city centre is also called the *English Market*. Fruit and veg come from organic agriculture, poultry and meat from organic farms. Daily fresh salmon, langoustines and lobster are also available, as well as all different kinds of fish from the region and a large selection of mussels. What more could you ask for!? *Mon–Sat 8am–6pm | Victorian halls in the centre, between Grand Parade and St Patrick's Street (Princes Street) | www.englishmarket.ie*

MERCHANT'S QUAY

Numerous boutiques, department stores, cafés, music stores and other shops are housed in a skilfully restored warehouse on the river. The first floor has a self-service restaurant with café, a meeting place mostly for locals. The Dunnes and Debenhams department stores are right next door. *St Patrick's Bridge | www.merchants quaycork.com*

Cork City Market is housed in Victorian halls

ENTERTAINMENT

AN BODHRÁN

Small pub with stylish old-fashioned interior. Live music five times a week. *42 Oliver Plunkett Street*

AN SPAILPÍN FÁNAC

Busy, cosy pub, with near-daily traditional music. At weekends in particular, students and tourists come together here. *27–29 South Main Street*

CORK OPERA HOUSE

A glass building filled with culture: the programme features opera, theatre and dance, but also musicals, revues, children's theatre and comedy. *Emmet Place | tel. 021 4270022 | www.cork operahouse.ie*

DAN LOWREY'S

Classy and stylish Irish pub with English elegance; pretty glass décor, fancy furnishings. *13 MacCurtain Street*

EVERYMAN PALACE THEATRE

The resident ensemble puts on mostly modern and classic Irish plays. *15 MacCurtain Street | tel. 021 4501673 | www.everymanpalace.com*

FRED ZEPPELINS

'Keep on rocking in the free world!' is the motto they follow at 'Freds', including live music. *8 Parliament Street | off South Mall*

THE MUTTON LANE INN

In the city's oldest (1787) and most beautiful pub – if a bit dingy and with an alternative touch – you can do more than just have a pint. The place puts on exhibitions of local artists and jam sessions on Monday. *3 Mutton Lane | off St Patrick's Street (next to English Market)*

SIN È

In this popular traditional pub – 'That's it' – you can hear 'Dirty Old Town' and 'Wicklow Hills' as well as unknown stuff: several times a week, there is traditional Irish live music. *8 Coburg Street*

INSIDER TIP ▶ TRISKEL CHRISTCHURCH

What was once the centre of Cork in the middle ages is now a stage for concerts, films, live music, theatre. Book readings take place in its adjoining Arts Centre and many big names perform here, like The Celtic Tenors or the folk singer Andy Irvine. Check out their programm to see what's on! *Tobin Street | tel. 021 4 27 20 22 | www.triskelartscentre.ie*

WHERE TO STAY

INSIDER TIP ▶ ASHLEY HOTEL

A great, affordable hotel with few downsides. As a guest, you'll sleep in a well-kept Victorian building from 1840. It's close to the city centre and the staff are friendly. Enjoy an Irish breakfast in the morning and a glass of Murphy's in the evening. The hotel bar is popular and brightly furnished. *Coburg Street | 27 rooms | tel. 021 4501518 | www.ashley hotel.com | Moderate*

CORK INTERNATIONAL HOSTEL

Large Victorian brick house near the university and Fitzgerald Park; the city centre is just over a mile's walk. *96 beds | 1/2 Redclyffe/Western Road | tel. 021 4543289 | Budget*

GARNISH HOUSE

Pretty *bed & breakfast* accommodation opposite the university and near Fitzgerald Park, pleasant atmosphere and reliable service. Close to the centre. *28 rooms | 18 Western Road/Donovan's Road | tel. 021 4275111 | www.garnish.ie | Moderate*

There is a near-Mediterranean atmosphere about Bantry House and its surroundings

HAYFIELD MANOR

Living like the Irish landed gentry: beautifully located in a park, just over a mile outside the city centre. The manor house spoils its guests with exquisitely designed rooms, several excellent restaurants and a spa with an outdoor jacuzzi. Sophisticated touches include the lavish five-o'clock tea and sherry in the library. Enjoy! *83 rooms | Perrott Av./College Road | tel. 021 4 84 95 00 | www.hayfieldmanor. ie | Expensive*

KILLARNEY GUEST HOUSE

Charming house dating back to 1847, yet all rooms en-suite, very comfortable and friendly. Parking available. *19 rooms | 59 Western Road | opposite the university | tel. 021 4 27 02 90 | www.killarneyguest house.com | Moderate*

KINLAY HOUSE

This hostel prides themselves on service! Not only do they offer dorms, but also double rooms with en-suite facilities. Free breakfast up to 9.30am, 24-hour service, kitchen, phone, internet access. Plus extras such as laundry service and bike storage. *104 beds | Bob and Joan's Walk | Shandon | tel. 021 4 50 89 66 | www.kinlayhousecork.ie | Budget*

METROPOLE

This centennial hotel with a slightly crumbling elegance lies on the northern bank of the river. Both pubs have singing in the evening, breakfast is taken with a view of the river. Nearby: a large leisure centre and several good restaurants. *98 rooms | MacCurtain Street | tel. 021 4 64 37 00 | www.metropolehotel.ie | Expensive*

INFORMATION

TOURIST OFFICE
42 Grand Parade | tel. 021 4 25 51 00 | www.discoverireland.ie

BALTIMORE (137 D6) (*Ⓜ C17*)

Heading southwest from Cork for a good 97 km/60 mi leads through picturesque river valleys and undulating hills to the romantic coast. Starting from Cork you first hit Clonakilty, where you can overnight at *O'Donovan's Hotel (26 rooms | Pearse Street | tel. 023 8 33 32 50 | www. odonovanshotel.com | Moderate)*, then Skibbereen before reaching Baltimore, the gateway to the islands of *Sherkin* and Cape *Clear*. The small port town of Baltimore awakens in the spring, with the arrival of sailing and fishing visitors. During the *Baltimore Fiddle Fair (www.fiddlefair. com)* at the start of May, there's *traditional and modern music.* If you miss the Sherkin Ferry *(hourly | crossing 15 min | 12 euros return | www.sherkinisland.eu/ ferry)* or the Cape Clear Ferry *(two to three times a day | 45 min | 16 euros return | www.cailinoir.com)*, you can stay overnight in Baltimore, e.g. in the imaginatively restored farmhouse *Rolf's Country House (10 rooms | The Hill | tel. 028 2 02 89 | rolfscountryhouse.com | Budget–Moderate)*.

BANTRY (137 D5) (*Ⓜ C17*)

In Bantry (92 km/57 mi west, pop. 2800), ● *Bantry House (house and garden open to the public, April/May/Sept/Oct Tue–Sun 10am–5pm, June–Aug daily 10am–5pm | admission 11 euros | Hotel 8 rooms | Expensive | tel. 027 5 00 47 | www.bantryhouse. ie)* is worth a detour. The pretty castle was purchased in 1739 by the ancestors of the current owners. Over time, it was furnished with stylish wall hangings, paintings and furniture. Italianate terraced gardens with fountains and statues surround the estate. There is a café and crafts shop. Two guest wings allow you to stay overnight in style – with the family at hand, and a round of croquet after breakfast.

BLARNEY CASTLE ★ ⚜
(137 F4) (*Ⓜ E16*)

9 km/5.5 mi west of Cork, the stronghold erected by Cormac McCarthy in 1446 dominates a park. The castle was restored to allow visitors to reach the famous *Blarney Stone* at 29 m/95 ft up, and after a fair bit of squiggling, to kiss it. Nearly everybody does that too, as the stone is said to lend the kisser the gift of the gab – *blarney* of course, meaning 'chatter, bla'. Walking trails lead from the castle into a park that has a flower garden called *Rock Close,* boasting rock formations considered to have a mythical significance. In summer, the Big House is open to visitors. *Park and castle 9am–5pm, in summer till 7pm | admission 15 euros | www.blarneycastle.ie* The pretty little village of *Blarney (www. blarney.com)* is best known for the souvenirs sold from the *Woollen Mills* shop in a restored factory.

CAPE CLEAR (136 C6) (*C18*)

Lonely Ireland: fewer than 200 people live on this small island ('Oileán Chléire' in Irish) a good 96 km/60 mi southwest of Cork (ferry from Baltimore). *St Kieran's Stone* stands at the well, and there is a shrine for the island's patron saint of the

Break for coffee in Cobh

same name. A steep path leads from the mooring up to the 12th-century ⚓ *St Kieran's Church*. To find further prehistoric monoliths, head for the eastern side of the island and *St Comillane*. The western coast boasts the ruined *O'Driscoll's Cas-*

tle dating back to the 14th century. *www. oilean-chleire.ie*

CASTLETOWNSHEND (137 D6) (*D17*)

The small settlement on Castle Haven Bay, 96 km/60 mi southwest of Cork, boasts an architectural gem: erected in the 17th century, the *Bow Hall* manor house has been converted into a guesthouse by Americans. Get a glimpse of village history at the *St Barrahane* church with its romantic ancient cemetery: Somerville, Coghill, Chavasse and Townshend — influential families that have been in this area for centuries.

Mary Anne's pub the steep main street has already been lauded in the New York Times — and rightly so. When it's sunny, you can sit in the courtyard and enjoy fabulous fish and seafood. The old *castle* in an overgrown park on the sea is still inhabited by the descendants of the founders. They rent out rooms in the castle and the adjacent cottages: *Castletownshend Guesthouse (The Castle | 11 rooms | tel. 028 36100 | www.castle-townshend. com | Budget)*.

COBH (138 A5–6) (*F16*)

The pretty port town on an island in extensive Cork Harbour, some 26 km/14 mi southeast of Cork, is connected with the mainland by a bridge. Up to 1950, it was from Cobh that ocean liners took Irish emigrants to America. Many houses still date back to the heyday of shipping in the 19th century. ⚓ *St Colman's* Gothic cathedral dominates the colourful houses from its steep plateau; its famous *glockenspiel* (47 bells) attracts many visitors. A boat trip of the harbour opens up the beauty of the place. Find out more about Cobh's history at the *Heritage Centre (daily 9.30am–6pm | admission 9.50 euros | tel. 021 4813591 | www.cobhheritage. com)* in the old Victorian train station.

FOTA ISLAND (138 A5) (*F16*)

Cross a bridge to reach Fota Island, har-bouring the *Fota Estate (April–Sept daily 9am–5pm | www.fotahouse.com)* where you can visit the *Manor House (admission 8 euros).* Behind the house, you'll find an *Arboretum.* In the skillfully land-scaped park, you'll see massive trees, rare plants and tropical rarities. Ap-proach: *From Cork, head towards Midleton and then turn right*

SCHULL (136 C6) (*C17*)

The lively market town *(www.schull.ie)* 109 km/68 mi southwest of Cork is a pop-ular holiday village with bed & breakfasts and holiday apartments, as well as the jetty for the Cape Clear ferry with a pro-tected harbour. Right on the pier, you can buy fish, fresh off the trawler or smoked. Shops and cafés line Schull's (also Skull's) main street. You'll discover exceptional arts and crafts work at Courtyard Crafts *(Main Street | www.courtyardcraftsonline. com).* Check out *Paradise Crèpe Restau-rant (Main Street | tel. 087 7 43 74 27 | Budget–Moderate).* They serve a lot more than just crêpes on their terrace and in their flower-filled garden. Along with the holiday village atmosphere, you also find an INSIDER TIP alternative side in Schull: esoteric and new age shops, vegan res-taurants, meditation centres and Far East alternative practitioners.

SHERKIN ISLAND
(137 D6) (*C18*)

The island a good 96 km/60 mi south-west of Cork is a great place for walks with views of the Atlantic. Archaeologi-cally minded visitors can discover prehis-toric rocks at *Slievemore* on the western side of the island and descend into Early Christian caves. The *Silver Strand* beach is the place to go for swimming. Anoth-er great place for photos are the ruins of a Franciscan monastery (1460). If you're looking for seclusion, head for the north-ern shore. *Daily ferries from Baltimore*

WEST CORK GARDEN TRAIL ●

(136–137 C5–D6) (*C–D17*)

Between Kinsale and Glengarriff, there are a number of gardens that the own-er has put together and called *West Cork Garden Trail.* A Japanese Kasuga lantern several metres high marks the entrance to the *Lassanaroe Garden* in the small fishing village of Skibbereen to prepare visitors for its extraordinary collection of rare types of bamboo. In the same village Lord and Lady Pultnam open their *Riv-er House Garden* with a Japanese boat-house, orchids and rare plants from the

DOG RACING

On nine state-run courses, gracious grey-hounds hare after a fake rabbit, six dogs in each of the eight to ten races that are held each evening. Nobody dresses up: fashion takes a back seat here. Some of the many small betting shops are one-man shows, whose owners take bets standing on beer crates. Visitors pay 10 euros to get in and place a bet (stakes of 5 euros) on the winner. All larger towns have racecourses, e.g. in Cork the ● *Curraheen Park Greyhound Stadium (Wed/Thu/Sat 7pm | Curraheen Park | Cur-raheen Road (off the N 25), 4,8 km/3 mi southwest of Cork city centre | (*)01890 26 99 69 (*) | www.igb.ie | bus 8).*

Himalayas. Not all gardens are open all year round, some only open their gates by previous appointment. Two weeks in June however, all gardens are open, staging special events. *www.westcork gardentrail.com*

YOUGHAL ★ (142 B5) (*🕮 F16*)

The pretty town of Youghal (pop. 6000) is situated on the estuary of the Blackwater River, a good 48 km/30 mi east of Cork. The arch of a four-storey clock tower (1777) spans the main street. Climb up the steep steps to the ☀ city wall, with foundations dating back to the 13th century. From up here you get good views across the town with many 18th- and 19th-century houses.

The path along the city wall passes several defensive towers, before arriving at *St Mary's Church*. Also dating from the 13th century, this stone-built church is well preserved. Said to have been founded as early as 450, the interior of the church is a treasure trove for those interested in Irish history!

Below the church, the (private) *Myrtle Grove* was one of the residences of Sir Walter Raleigh (who is credited with bringing the potato to Ireland). If you have time, head for the harbour *(Market Square)* to visit the *Court House*, the elongated *Market House* as well as the *Water Gate*.

KILLARNEY

(136–137 C–D4) (*🕮 C16*) **There's no doubt about it: the most beautiful thing about Killarney is the nature around it. Lying in a valley, the town is framed by three lakes: Lough Leane, Muckross Lake and Lough Guitane.**

Numerous rivers feed the waters amidst the near-evergreen vegetation. The backdrop is formed by several peaks, amongst them the *Macgillycuddy's Reeks*, at 1041 m/3412 ft Ireland's highest mountain. The fabulously beautiful landscape, a great national park, as well as Muckross House, a classy manor house, have made Killarney (pop. 14,500) what it is today: a thoroughly commercialised tourist town. Each year during the short summer season, holidaymakers flood into the town, creating logjams already outside the town's limits. At least cars are banned from Killarney's town centre in summer between 7pm and 8am. ● There is no escaping the *jaunting cars*, whose drivers shout out offers for sightseeing drives to destinations inside Killarney National Park.

SIGHTSEEING

GAP OF DUNLOE

Cliffs, lakes and green mountains dominate the broad gorge running between the MacGillycuddy's Reeks to the west and Purple Mountain to the east at the exit of Killarney National Park. The starting point of a popular hike is the historic *Kate Kearney's Cottage (www.katekear neyscottage.com)* with pub and restaurant. From here a narrow road winds through a rough rocky near-alpine landscape. The horse-and-cart outfits take about an hour for the 9 km/5.5-mi tour leading past three lakes (Black Lake, Cushnavalley Lake and Auger Lake).

MUCKROSS HOUSE ★

Built in 1843 by Scottish architect William Burn in the Victorian style for the Herbert family in an idyllic location on the shores of Muckross Lake, Muckross House is the country's most famous manor house. In 1964 it was made accessible to the public. Alongside rooms serving as a folk museum and to display old skills and crafts (weaving, pottery, blacksmithing), the rest of the castle-like mansion is kept in the style of around 1900 *(daily 9am–6pm | admission incl. guided tour 9 euros | 5 km/3 mi south on the N 71 | www.muckross-house.ie)*. Access to Muckross House through the park is pretty all year round, but particularly spectacular in May when the rhododendrons are in bloom. The surrounding *Killarney National Park* (several entrances) offers fabulous hikes, to the ruined 15th-century monastery of *Muckross Abbey* for instance, to *Torc Waterfall* and the *Old Weir Bridge* (signposted). The area of the national park, spanning about 25,000 acres, was handed over to the state in 1932, together with Muckross House. Today, the park boasting Ireland's largest oak forest is under Unesco protection as a biosphere reserve. Get more information (also on guided walks) at the tourist information centre in Killarney or at *www.killarneynationalpark.ie*.

ROSS CASTLE

Built in the 15th century, this impressive castle features two round towers, strong defensive walls and antique oak furniture. Pretty lakeside location. *March–Oct 9.30am–5.30pm | admission 5 euros | Ross Road | Bay of Ross, Lower Lake | 1.9 km/1.2 mi southwest of Killarney*

FOOD & DRINK

GABY'S SEAFOOD

Being small didn't stop this fine fish restaurant from receiving the 'Irish Seafood Award'. The house speciality is lobster – fresh from one of the tanks. *Mon–Sat 6pm–10pm | 27 High Street | tel. 064 6 63 25 19 | Expensive*

Muckross House: Discover the splendour of the Victorian era

MAC'S
Changing lunch menu, including fish, chicken, pasta and grill dishes as well as 30 flavours of ice cream. *Thu–Sun 10.30am–10pm | 6 Main Street | tel. 064 6 63 52 13 | www.macsofmainstreet.com | Budget*

INSIDER TIP ▶ MUCKROSS GARDEN RESTAURANT
Chicken with Clonakilty black pudding or *apple pie* with vanilla ice cream straight from the oven – everything they serve here tastes good. Add to that the idyllic location at Muckross House: you can either sit in the rustic modern restaurant, the light-filled conservatory or – even better – on the terrace, furnished with teak chairs and tables. *Daily 9am–7pm | Muckross House, Killarney National Park | tel. 064 6 63 93 54 | Moderate*

SMOKE HOUSE
A lively and tasteful environment with the best food in town, e.g. the Kerry Lamb grilled over wood and the seasoned Steak Burger. Homemade and lushly prepared desserts. *Mon–Fri 5pm–10pm, Sat/Sun 12pm–10pm | 8 High Street | tel. 064 6 63 93 36 | Moderate*

SHOPPING

KILKENNY SHOP
A handwoven shawl made in Donegal or the teapot with its 70s-like, eccentric retro design? You'll find the finest Irish quality here – and that at fair prices. *3 New Street*

MR MCGUIRES OLDE SWEET SHOP
Old-Style Liquorice, Irish chocolate, brightly coloured lollies and surprise bags of sweets – a shop that could be out of a picture book. *College Square*

LEISURE & SPORTS

KILLARNEY BOATING & TOUR CENTRE
It's like a dream, floating through Killarney National Park on the *Lilly of Killarney Watercoach*. After seeing Ross Castle, hop on a boat for a one-hour discovery tour. Tickets available in the *Tourist Information Office (see p. 61). Daily 10.30am, noon, 1.45pm, 3.15pm, 4.30pm from Ross Castle | Tour costs 12 euros | Muckross Road | Old Weir Lodge | tel. 064 6 63 10 68 | www.killarneydaytour.com*

KILLARNEY RIDING STABLES
Alongside horses, the stables also offer accommodation in the farmhouse and trail riding over several days. Founded in 1968, this farm next to the National Park now holds 70 horses for riders to choose from. *Ballydowney | 1.9 km/1.2 mi west of town on the N 72 | tel. 064 6 63 16 86 | www.killarney-riding-stables.com*

ENTERTAINMENT

SHEEHAN'S
In the evenings, the Killarney Grand hotel's own traditional pub is buzzing with Irish folk and traditional dance from 9pm. *Main Street | tel. 064 6 63 11 59 | www.killarneygrand.com*

WHERE TO STAY

EARLS COURT HOUSE
Fine guesthouse decorated in 19th-century style on the edge of town towards Muckross. Romantics will love the interior: some of the rooms have a fireplace and four-poster bed. Opulent breakfast. *30 rooms | Woodlawn Junction Muckross Road | tel. 064 6 63 40 09 | www.killarney-earlscourt.ie | Moderate*

THE EUROPE HOTEL & RESORT ●

For lovers of design and nature: panoramic windows make the sea and the mountains become one with the spacious lobby; the gleaming chrome bar is reminiscent of Philippe Starck, the library a cave clad in black, with precious coffee-table books, and the Spa Centre with huge pool the most beautiful in the entire region. *187 rooms | Fossa | N 72 to Killorglin, 4.8 km/3 mi west of Killarney | tel. 064 6 671300 | www.theeurope.com | Moderate*

GLENA HOUSE

A pretty *bed & breakfast* with a bistro-style restaurant, tea and coffee-making facilities in the room and a car park. Just a five-minute walk to the centre of town. *29 rooms | 23 Muckross Road | tel. 064 6 6379 33 | www.harmonyinn.ie| Budget*

KILLARNEY PARK HOTEL ☟

At this five-star country house, enjoy the coffee from silver pots with a view of the mountains and historic Killarney, *afternoon tea* at the open fire or treatments at the spa. *68 rooms | Town Centre | East Avenue Road | tel. 064 6 63 55 55 | www. killarneyparkhotel.ie | Expensive*

INFORMATION

TOURIST INFORMATION OFFICE
Beech Road | off New Street | tel. 064 6 63 16 33 | www.killarney.ie

WHERE TO GO

BEARA PENINSULA
(136 B6–C5) (𝄐 B17–C16)
Jutting out into the sea between Bantry Bay and Kenmare, south of the Ring of

Bliss on a boat: the best way to discover Killarney National Park

Kerry, the harsh and wild Beara Peninsula awaits. The road snaking along the peninsula, the INSIDER**TIP** *Ring of Beara* is much less busy than the more popular routes around the Ring of Kerry and Dingle.

Following the Tibetan-Buddhist tradition, the excellent ● *Dzogchen Beara* meditation centre (*Garranes | Allihies | tel. 027 73032 | www.dzogchenbeara.org | Budget*) sits above dramatic coastal cliffs and is open to interested visitors. There are free guided meditations on a daily basis (9am–9.45am) and weekend retreats (200 euros incl. food). In the cute café, you'll enjoy the wholefood cake and chocolate muffins just as much as the conversation with the centre's owners.

On the southwest point of the peninsula, the 🚠 INSIDER**TIP** *Dursey Cable Car* (*daily 9am–7.30pm | crossing 8 euros return | Windy Point House | Allihies*) takes visitors onto Dursey Island, a trip of 374 m/1227 ft. The island, covering 4 by 1 miles, has only a handful of inhabitants, no pub, guesthouse or restaurant. A 11 km/7 mi hiking trail, allowing you to spot many seabirds, leads past the lighthouse and around the island. In the summer, there's a bus (*www.durseyisland.ie*)

INSIDER**TIP** **BLASKET ISLANDS** (136 A3) (*Ø A15*)
Up until 1953, these islands were inhabited by an Irish-speaking community that published over a dozen books. Some of them are available at the *Blasket Centre* (*admission 5 euros | Dunquin*). Boat tours with the chance to see whales, dolphins and seals (*4 hours | daily 1pm | 50 euros*) and tours to the Blasket Islands (*4 hours stay | daily 10am–5pm | 60 euros*) from Ventry through *Eco Marine Adventure Tour (tel. 086 3 35 38 05 | www.marine tours.ie). 88 km/55 mi west of Killarney*

INSIDER**TIP** **DINGLE** (136 B3) (*Ø B15*)
Although this fishing town's (pop. 2000) colourful, charming and small, it's still the capital of the Dingle Peninsula and mustn't be underestimated. It has excellent restaurants and the people in the pubs are always in high spirits. You may be tempted to stay here a few days – perhaps in the bright red *Dingle Bay Hotel* (*25 rooms | Strand Street | tel. 066 915 1231 | www.dinglebayhotel.com | Moderate*). It's located on the harbour and conveniently placed in the middle of everything around. The 30 km/18.6 mi-long *Slea Head Drive* has tons of curves, but the views over the wild Atlantic are spectacular. The road leads to a promontory called *Slea Head*. It boasts a beach so secluded and beautiful that David Lean used it as a backdrop in his film 'Ryan's Daughter'.

GLENGARRIFF (136 C5) (*Ø C17*)
Palm trees and fuchsia hedges adorn the village (pop. 800) on the estuary where

the Glengarriff River flows into Bantry Bay; plenty of tourists visit during the summer months. The terrace café of the Victorian *Eccles Hotel (66 rooms | Glengarriff Harbour | tel. 027 6 30 03 | www. eccleshotel.com | Moderate)* affords a view of Glengarriff Bay. Right opposite the hotel, the *Harbour Queen (One trip: 15 euros | April–Oct | www.harbourqueen-ferry.com)* leaves every 20 minutes and takes you over to *Garinish Island (www. garnishisland.com)*. Covering 37 acres, this island is famous for its Mediterranean garden architecture with Greek temples, tree ferns reaching 2 m/2,2 yd and rare subtropical trees.

RING OF KERRY
(140 B–C 3–5) (*ᆱ B–C 15–16*)

The famous Ring of Kerry is a unique coastal and panoramic road leading for some 201 km/125 mi around the Iveragh Peninsula. The road is so narrow that buses are only allowed to use it driving in one direction. In order to properly enjoy the sublime landscape, try and schedule at least two days for a visit. Fabulous views across ᨏ *Dingle Bay* open up on the section between Glenbeigh and Cahersiveen.

The fishing village of Glenbeigh, 12 km/ 7.5 mi west of Killorglin, is the starting point for trekking and hiking routes across the Macgillycuddy's Reeks and around Caragh Lake. A lovely ᨏ hiking tour leads from Seefin in a semicircle to Drung Hill. It goes through a fantastic landscape of lakes and hills with panoramic sea views. Beach life can be enjoyed at Rossbeigh Beach. Overnight accommodation is available at the *Olde Glenbeigh Hotel (12 rooms | tel. 066 9 76 83 33 | www.glenbeighhotel.com | Moderate)*.

From Portmagee, a bridge leads to *Valentia Island,* a place of huge fuchsias,

Spectacular views of the Dingle Peninsula's steep coastline

rhododendrons and brambles, with wide plains in between. *Knightstown*, the island's largest town and starting point for fishing and diving tours, has a fairly sleepy vibe. A paradise for anglers on the mainland is *Waterville*, which lies as in a lagoon between the sea and a lake. Numerous hiking trails lead around *Lough Currane* and into the mountains beyond. At the southern start of the Ring of Kerry, Kenmare Bay, the pretty town of *Kenmare* (pop. 2500) features some limestone houses with lavish decoration. Fish restaurants and craft shops line the few streets. Needing a second break? On the peninsula's southern coast you'll find *Sneem (www.sneemireland.com)*. A pint of cider tastes amazing under the sun. Get yours while sitting in front of one of the charming restaurants or pubs. You're sure to never forget this place if you also decide to book a night at the *Parknasilla Resort (83 | 064 6 67 56 00 | www.park nasillaresort.com | Moderate–Expensive)*. Romance at its finest!

Visitors travelling by car and wanting to follow the Ring of Kerry by the Cliffs of Moher can save the detour via Limerick with the INSIDERTIP car ferry from Tarbert to Killimer *(7am–9pm half-hourly to hourly | crossing time 20 minutes | 19 euros per car incl. passengers | www.shan nonferries.com)*.

SKELLIG MICHAEL★ (136 A5) (*Ш A16*)

12 km/7.5 mi off the coast, you'll reach ☆ Skellig Michael (also called *Great Skellig*). Rising steeply from the sea, this island planet is known by Star Wars fans as Ahch-To, Luke Skywalker's place of retreat. Difficult to reach from the mainland, this island boasts an 8th-century monastic settlement which sits majestically at its peak. Once occupied for 600 years, it's now a Unesco World Heritage Site. 670 steps take you to the top which offers sheer breathtaking views. A little closer to the coast, the neighbouring island of *Little Skellig* shelters the world's second-largest gannet colony. There are boat services between the mainland and Skellig Michael (the crossing is dependent on the weather!). The boat circles Little Skellig but is not allowed to land there. Departure from Portmagee and Knightstown. The *boat tours (June–Sept daily (depends on the weather) 9am–2pm | price: 50 euros | April–Oct eco tour circling both islands (without landing) daily 14.30pm–16.30pm | price: 30 euros | www.skelligis

lands.com) start in Portmagee. Exhibition on the islands: *Skellig Experience Centre (Island Bridge, Valentia Island | March/April/Oct/Nov Mon–Fri 10am–5pm, May/June/Sept daily 10am–6pm, July/Aug until 7pm | admission 5 euros, round trip 30 euros | tel. 066 9 47 63 06 | www.skellig experience.com)*.

KINSALE

(137 F5) (*Ш E17*) ★ This is a picture-postcard kind of a place: Kinsale is an all-round pretty port (pop. 4000) with colourful rows of houses along narrow winding streets, a flower-bedecked seafront promenade and sailing yachts in the harbour.

In the sports and society calendar, the sailing regatta in August is the top event in the region. The rest of the time, Kinsale attracts visitors to its numerous pubs and excellent if pricey restaurants. The town prides itself on being Ireland's culinary capital.

SIGHTSEEING

CHARLES FORT ☆

A pleasant one-hour walk of almost 3,2 km/2 mi along the bay on the eastern side of the harbour through Scilly and Summercove leads to the British fort. The imposing star-shaped fortification from the year 1677 is well preserved. On the other side of the bridge, you'll see *James Fort (1602)*. *Summercove*

KINSALE REGIONAL MUSEUM

In the former courthouse (1706), displays bring to life the town's history from megalithic settlement to the Battle of Kinsale fought by the British against the Spanish. *Sat 10am–5pm, Sun 2–5pm | free admission | Old Court House | Market Square*

ST MULTOSE

This church built in the 12th century by the Normans is the town's oldest building. The cemetery shelters some of the 1198 victims of the Lusitania disaster. The torpedoing of a passenger liner by a German U-boat in 1915 triggered America's entry into the First World War. *Church Street*

FOOD & DRINK

FISHY FISHY RESTAURANT

Some say this is the best fish restaurant in Ireland, and there really is excellent seafood here, including smoked salmon with shrimp sandwiches and fresh brown soda bread. If you want to make the dishes at home, the owner Martin Shanahan sells his 'Irish Seafood Cookery Book' inside. *Daily 12pm–9pm | Crowleys Quay | tel. 021 4 70 04 15 | www.fishyfishy.ie | Moderate*

PIER ONE

Views across the harbour, daily changing menu and fresh fish every day. *Daily 8–11am and 6.30–9pm | at the Trident Hotel | World's End | tel. 021 4 77 93 00 | www.tridenthotel.com | Moderate*

TODDIES AT THE BULMAN

Contemporary Irish cuisine (local fish specialities and crustaceans) with harbour views. The ground floor is occupied by a 200-year-old pub; in the summer life moves outside. *Daily 12.30pm–5pm, Tue–Sat 6pm–9pm | Summercove | tel. 021 4 77 21 31 | www.thebulman.ie | Moderate*

SHOPPING

GRANNY'S BOTTOM DRAWER

Irish linen and Aran sweaters of excellent quality. Decoratives for your house and garden are also sold. *53 Main Street*

The building façades in Kinsale: Picture perfect!

LEISURE & SPORTS

KINSALE HARBOUR CRUISES
Board the *Spirit of Kinsale* for a trip around the harbour, past the fort and the Old Town. *Daily departures from the quay between Actons Hotel (300 m/984 ft) and the marina | timetable at tourist office | 13 euros | www.kinsaleharbourcruises.com*

OUTDOOR EDUCATION CENTRE
Sailing, windsurfing, canoe tours, mountaineering, free climbing, discovering nature and much more, classes for beginners and advanced levels. *St John's Hill | tel. 021 4 77 28 96 | www.kinsaleoutdoors.com*

ENTERTAINMENT

THE SPANIARD
Everything is just so in this self-styled *olde worlde inn of character and charm*. Located above the harbour, this cosily furnished pub restaurant is a meeting place for young and old. Delicious dishes include *seafood chowder* and *bacon & cabbage*. *Scilly | tel. 021 4 77 24 36 | www.thespaniard.ie*

WHERE TO STAY

ACTONS HOTEL
Classy, elegant, central and right on the harbour. One of the most popular hotels around. *73 rooms | Pier Road | tel. 021 4 77 99 00 | www.actonshotelkinsale.com | Moderate*

OLD BANK HOUSE
This Georgian townhouse is the most stylish amongst Kinsale's luxury hotels. The cosy rooms have a very personal touch, furnished with antiques, paintings, and plush upholstery. *17 rooms | 11 Pearse Street | tel. 021 4 77 40 75 | www.oldbankhousekinsale.com | Expensive*

TIERNEY'S GUESTHOUSE
Welcoming rooms in a Georgian townhouse. Their excellent *Irish breakfast* is served in the conservatory. *10 rooms | 70 Main Street | tel. 021 4 77 22 05 | www.tierneys-kinsale.com | Budget*

TRIDENT ☆
A quarrystone building with a fresh design and top location. You'll have a great view of the fishing trawlers and sailing boats. *64 rooms | World's End | tel. 021 4 77 93 00 | www.tridenthotel.com | Moderate*

INFORMATION

TOURIST OFFICE
Emmet Place | tel. 021 4 77 22 34 | www.kinsale.ie

LIMERICK

MAP INSIDE THE BACK COVER
(137 F1) (🗺 E14) Since millions of euros were spent in recuperating and restoring public buildings, and the opening of new chic hotels, restaurants and shops, Ireland's third-largest city (pop. 91,000) exudes a new self-confidence.

Limerick also happens to be the country's oldest settlement. The Normans erected city walls and castles and constructed a bridge across the Shannon. In the 18th century, Limerick was given its current aspect: with broad streets and imposing townhouses in the Georgian style. A few miles north of the city, Shannon Airport is handy for visitors wanting to travel the southwest of Ireland, as well as Galway and the Shannon region.

SIGHTSEEING

HUNT MUSEUM

Among the highlights in this small yet fine museum are drawings by Picasso and paintings by Renoir and Gauguin. This outstanding collection is a unique private art collection comprising around 2000 exhibits, including even some from the Bronze and Iron Age. The art is presented on three floors of the Palladian-style Customs House. In the basement, you'll find a tea room and well-decorated shop. *Mon–Sat 10am–5pm, Sun 2–5pm | admission 5 euros | Rutland Street | www.huntmuseum.com*

KING JOHN'S CASTLE

Built in the early 13th century by the Normans on the banks of the river Shannon, the castle used to have four round tow-

> **WHERE TO START?**
> **Patrick Street:** stroll from here to King John's Castle via a tributary of the River Shannon. If arriving by hire car, the best place to park is at Arthur's Quay in front of the tourist office on the River Shannon. Trains arrive at Colbert Station, a few minutes on foot from the city centre.

ers, one of which was subsequently converted into the bastion. Today, steps replace the former drawbridge. The castle was re-opened in 2013 after extensive renovations. *Daily 9.30am–17.30pm, May–Sept till 7.30pm | admission 8 euros | Castle Parade | King's Island | off Nicholas Street*

The evening sun turns the stone walls of King John's Castle on the River Shannon golden

INSIDER TIP **WALKING TOURS**

Take an entertaining and historical walk through the city with Declan, a charming insider from Limerick. The tour is offered by *Limerick Walking Tours (tour 10 euro | www.limerickwalkingtours.com)*. Get more information at the Tourist Office. Hear typical stories related to Ireland. The Irish have great fun telling them.

FOOD & DRINK

FREDDY'S BISTRO

Italian and Irish cuisine in a stylish building of natural stone; also vegetarian. Recommended: the *Irish Guinness stew*. *Tue–Sun 5.30pm–11pm | Theatre Lane | off Lower Glentworth Street | tel. 061 41 87 49 | www.freddysbistro.com | Expensive*

THE GLEN TAVERN

Traditional Irish Stew and classic dishes served in an 18th-century. From spring to fall, you can sit under the awning outside. In the evening, regulars come and order pint after pint. *Daily | 2 Lower Glentworth Street | Budget*

SHOPPING

IRISH HANDCRAFTS

Family-run operation specialising in tweed, fine linen and unusual woven textiles. *26 Patrick Street | www.irish handcraft.com*

ENTERTAINMENT

DOLAN'S PUB & THE WAREHOUSE

Unexpected performances set the mood with traditional music in *Dolan's Pub*. In the *Warehouse* nextdoor there are concerts and clubbing events. *Start usually 9pm | tickets 5–20 euros | 3–4 Dock Road | tel. 061 31 44 83 | www. dolanspub.com*

Typical thatched cottages in Adare village

WHERE TO STAY

CASTLETROY PARK

This large (20 m/66 ft-long!) indoor pool has everything you need to relax after a long day of sightseeing. Enjoy a steam bath, the sauna and the boxspring beds. You'll sleep like heaven here! *107 rooms | Dublin Road | tel. 061 33 55 66 | www. castletroypark.ie | Moderate–Expensive*

THE GEORGE

This city-centre boutique hotel embodies Limerick's new image: hip, artistic and international. Some of the rooms have an open fire. Guests meet for a pint in George's Bar. *124 rooms | O'Connell Street | tel. 061 46 04 00 | www.the georgeboutiquehotel.com | Moderate*

KILMURRY LODGE

Rustic country house atmosphere with a touch of Laura Ashley: this quiet genteel hotel is situated a bit outside the city, surrounded by extensive green spaces and close to the university. *100 rooms | Dublin Road | N 7 | Castletroy | tel. 061 33 11 33 | www.kilmurrylodge.com | Moderate*

INFORMATION

TOURIST OFFICE

20 O'Connell Street | tel. 061 317 5 22 | www.limerick.ie

WHERE TO GO

ADARE (141 E1) (ᴍ E14)

Thatched cottages, climbing roses and pleasant gardens dominate 'Ireland's prettiest village'. The Earls of Duraven built this village for their workers in the 19th-century. Some 18 km/11 mi southwest of Limerick, Adare (pop. 700) is now the place to go if you're looking to feast in style. The amazing ● *1826*

Adare (Wed–Sat from 6pm, Sun from 1pm | Main Street | 061 39 60 04 | www.1826adare.ie | Expensive) is one fine example. Here, Wade Murphy serves up scallops and lamb stew. The earls once resided in the *Adare Manor* with its Gothic arches, leaded windows and 75 chimneys. Today, it's Ireland's most romantic castle hotel. It's worth coming just for *5 o'clock tea*. There are good handicrafts at the *Adare Heritage Centre (daily 9am–6pm | free admission | Main Street | www.adareheritagecentre. ie)*. Here, you can also get tickets for a tour through *Desmond Castle (June–Sept | admission 5 euros, tour 9 euros)*. The ruins of this 13th-century castle are still impressive to see.

BUNRATTY CASTLE ● (137 E1) (ᴍ E13)

The restored castle some 16 km/10 mi northwest (on the N 18 in the direction of Ennis) has precious antique furniture. Twice a day *(5.30pm and 9pm)*, medieval banquets with musical accompaniment are put on. Extending immediately behind the castle, *Bunratty Folk Park* is a replica of an Irish 19th-century village. *Daily 9.30am–5.30pm (castle until 4pm) | admission 11.55 euros (castle and park)*

CRAGGAUNOWEN (137 D6) (ᴍ E13)

Some 30 km/19 mi northwest of the city, it is worth visiting the open-air museum with a Bronze Age settlement on an artificial island (*crannog*), a 5th-century ringfort with farmstead and the boat used by explorer Tim Severin for his 1976 sailing from Ireland to Greenland, in order to prove that the Celts could have discovered America before Columbus did. The imposing *Craggaunowen Castle* rises up on a crag above the lake. *April–Sept daily 10am–5pm | admission 9 euros*

THE WEST COAST

The west of Ireland is something special: the basalt and granite Cliffs of Moher dropping down into the ocean along a stretch of 8 km/5 mi. And the Burren, a rocky plateau with caves and subterranean corridors that many compare to a lunar landscape, fascinates visitors with its unique rare plants as well as testimonies to Early Christian times.

On the Aran Islands, a lonely cliff fort exudes a mythical atmosphere, while Connemara stands for charming coastal and mountainous landscapes. In Galway, the region also offers a typically Irish metropolis – a vibrant harbour city said by the Irish to have a Mediterranean flair. What you will certainly discover there is an exciting arts scene and much joie de vivre.

GALWAY

(132 C4) (*∅ D11*) Summer in Galway (pop. 79,000) is a time of festivities and events, whether the Galway Races in July or the Arts Festival, where the entire city becomes a mecca for the arts.

Come for the Galway Oyster Festival and help the locals wolf down the best oysters in Ireland with rivers of Guinness. Colourful old houses in the compact Old Town, friendly people, some of them even speaking Irish amongst themselves: Galway embodies Ireland in the nicest way, including the ability to bring together tradition and the 21st century. People from all over the world throng

Photo: Inishmore on the Aran Islands

Lunar landscapes and lakes teeming with fish. Discover unspoilt nature while biking, hiking or simply relaxing

the cafés and Eyre Square, so alongside traditional singing pubs and basic bed & breakfasts, there is an increasing selection of hip hotels and restaurants. Even the inevitable rain is said to be more fun in Galway than elsewhere.

SIGHTSEEING

COLLEGIATE CHURCH OF ST NICHOLAS
The country's largest medieval church dates back to the year 1320. According to legend, Columbus is said to have prayed here with his men before setting sail again for America. *Market Street*

GALWAY CITY MUSEUM ●
A new glass-fronted building show over 1000 exhibits to tell the story of a city that thousands of years old. Most were given to the museum by citizens of Galway. You'll have an excellent view of the city and harbour from the ☆ terrace. *Easter–Sept Tue–Sat 10am–5pm, Sun noon–5pm | free admission | Spanish Pa-*

The Quays: Music for all tastes and ages

rade at Spanish Arch | www.galwaycity museum.ie

KIRWAN'S LANE
The most beautiful medieval alley in Galway has been sensitively restored and is lined by shops, residential housing and restaurants. *Off Quay Street*

LYNCH'S MEMORIAL WINDOW
In 1493, Mayor James Lynch declared his son guilty of having killed a Spaniard out of jealousy. As nobody could be found who wanted to execute the son, the father took matters into his own hands – literally. Since this day, it is said that the vocabulary of the people of Galway, and later everybody else, acquired the expression 'lynching'. A window arch with memorial plaque in the wall of St Nicholas Church is a reminder of the event. *Market Street*

FOOD & DRINK

INSIDER TIP KAI CAFÉ RESTAURANT
This homely decorated building boasts stone walls and natural light thanks to its glass roof. From their menu, you can order fancy ✪ organic salads and sandwiches made with nutty wholemeal bread. Mmm! Delicious! *Café: Mon–Sat 9.30am–noon, Sun noon–3pm, Restaurant: Tue–Sat 6.30pm–10.30pm | Sea Road | tel. 091 52 60 03 | www.kaicafe restaurant.com | Budget–Moderate*

KIRWAN'S
Creative cuisine in the new Irish style. This place is way beyond cabbage & potatoes and located in a medieval alley. *Mon–Sat 12.30–2.30pm and 6–10pm, Sun 6–10pm | Kirwan's Lane | off Quay Street | tel. 091 56 82 66 | www. kirwanslane.com | Expensive*

MCDONAGH'S SEAFOOD HOUSE

Even the New York Times is full of praise: they have been serving up fish and sea-food – fresh off the boat and prepared in delicious ways, in an imposing seafood platter, for example – since 1902. For a cheaper option, choose the attached fish & chips bar. *Mon–Sat noon–11pm, Sun 2pm–9pm | 22 Quay Street | tel. 091 56 50 01 | www.mcdonaghs.net | Budget*

INSIDER TIP **MORAN'S OYSTER COTTAGE**

A 30-minute drive that is worth every minute. The centre of the oyster culture is located in this lovely cottage along the Kilcolgan River. This is a cult address for Gourmets. Especially delicious is the *Grilled Wild Native Oysters* with *Garlic Breadcrumbs*. *Daily noon–11.30pm | The Weir | 20 km/12.5 mi southeastern, N 18 | tel. 091 79 6113 | www.moransoyster cottage.com | Moderate*

SHOPPING

JUDY GREENE

Irish crafts and design: glassware, jewellery, ceramics, china, small items of home furniture and fabrics. You'll also be wonderfully advised. *Kirwan's Lane | www.judygreenepottery.com*

TWICE AS NICE

Irish linen and hand-made lace (in the shape of tableware and bedlinen as well as clothing) are for sale in this colourful Old Townhouse. Also soaps made to old recipes, jewellery and antiques. *5 Quay Street | www.twiceasniceireland.com*

LEISURE & SPORTS

SALTHILL PROMENADE

On this 2.5 km/1.5 mi-long walk, you'll be surrounded by the wind and waves. This wide promenade leads to Salthill where you can take a break in one of its many cosy cafés and pubs.

ENTERTAINMENT

INSIDER TIP **THE QUAYS**

Pub with several bar areas. The cosy interior has a maritime touch and Gothic arches. Students gather in the *Old Bar* on the ground floor for traditional music. Upstairs you'll hear Dixie, rock and other styles of music. *11 Quay Street | tel. 091 56 83 47*

INSIDER TIP **RÓISÍN DUBH**

This near-legendary pub is known for its Irish rock'n'roll scene. You'll even see past greats pop up here from time to time. There are always live concerts, amongst them blues and folk, too. *8 Upper Dominick Street | tel. 091 58 65 40 | www.roisindubh.net*

★ **Aran Islands**
Three old-fashioned islands with Ireland's most beautiful ring fort right on the cliff edge → p. 74

★ **Burren**
Bare landscape with arctic plants, exciting caves and subterranean rivers → p. 75

★ **Cliffs of Moher**
What an amazing coast! Rocky cliffs jut up 650 ft from the sea and touch the Irish sky. Wow! → p. 76

★ **Connemara**
Beaches on a fantastic coast, waterfalls – an undiluted nature experience for hikers → p. 76

MARCO POLO HIGHLIGHTS

WHERE TO STAY

ARDILAUN HOUSE

Town palace dating back to 1840 and converted into a first-class hotel with pool and spa, tennis, squash, as well as pitch & putt. *125 rooms | Taylors Hill | tel. 091 52 14 33 | www.theardilaunhotel.ie | Moderate*

BARNACLE'S QUAY STREET HOUSE

From the pubs and shops of the pedestrian zone, it's only a few steps to the double rooms or dorms with 6–12 (bunk) beds. Guests gather in a large, naturally-lighted kitchen for their Continental breakfast. *112 beds | 10 Quay Street | tel. 091 56 86 44 | www.barnacles.ie | Budget*

THE G HOTEL

Candy colours and a spot of Baroque fused with a touch of minimalism – this luxury hotel likes to play with contrasts. Three interlocking lounges, a fabulous Asian-style spa across two floors with bamboo garden on the roof. *101 rooms | Dublin Road (R 338)/Wellpark | tel. 091 8 65 20 0 | www.theghotel.ie | Expensive*

PARK HOUSE

Cosy luxury in a restored historic house with generously sized rooms in strong colours. For the past 25 years, the restaurant has defended its position as one of the best in town. *84 rooms | Forster Street | near Eyre Square | tel. 091 56 49 24 | www.parkhousehotel.ie | Expensive*

SLEEPZONE HOSTEL

In the city centre: modern kitchen, terrace, launderette, 24-hour access. Single rooms, double rooms and dorms (6–8 beds). *197 beds | Bothar Na mBan | opposite Dyke Road | tel. 091 56 69 99 | www.sleepzone.ie | Budget*

THE WESTERN

Georgian guesthouse with large comfortable rooms and a popular pub. *40 rooms | 33 Prospect Hill | near Eyre Square | tel. 091 56 28 34 | www.thewestern.ie | Moderate*

INFORMATION

TOURIST OFFICE

Forster Street | near Eyre Square | tel. 091 53 77 00 | www.galwaytourism.com

WHERE TO GO

ARAN ISLANDS ★

(132 B4–5) (*Ø* C12)

Of the three Aran Islands – Inisheer, Inishmaan and Inishmore – lying opposite Galway Bay, the latter is the largest, covering some 48 km²/18 sq mi. The Aran Islands (pop. 1500) are known all over the country for their Celtic customs and as a stronghold of the Irish language. On the bare little islands, time seems to have stood still. Inishmore boasts ● *Dun Aengus,* the most important and most beautiful stone fort in Ireland, in a fantastically dramatic position on the edge of sheer cliffs. Some visitors go down on their bellies to inch forward right to the edge of the abyss: over 100 m/328 ft below, the Atlantic is battering against the rocks.

The islands are crisscrossed by skilfully layered stone walls that keep in the heat and protect from the wind – just as the famous Aran sweaters that are for sale everywhere – and here is a good place to get them. Guesthouses offer *bed & (full Irish) breakfast,* in the evening, life repairs to the pubs. *Daily ferry services from various ports, e.g. Doolin | www.doolin ferries.com; from Rossaveal | www.aran islandferries.com); flights with Aer Arann from the regional airport in Inverin | tel. 091 59 30 34 | www.aerarannislands.ie*

A good place to stay is the *Ostan Arann (Aran Islands Hotel) (22 rooms | tel. 099 61104 | www.aranislandshotel.com | Moderate)*, 400 m/1312 ft from the pier at Inishmore, a house clad in stone, with a restaurant and bar. ☆ **INSIDER TIP** Five balcony rooms have views of the bay and harbour. Right at the ferry terminal, you can rent bikes (10 euros/day) at *Aran Bike Hire (The Pier | Inishmore | Kilronan | tel. 099 61132 | www.aranislandsbike hire.com)*.

derground labyrinth of caves and rivers with numerous stalactites. Next to the cave, the *Burren Birds of Prey Centre (admission 10 euros)* breeds and rears falcons, eagles, owls and other birds of prey.

A reminder of Ireland's early history, when the Burren was still inhabited, are *ring forts* (circular walls of stone or soil) and *dolmens* (large stone 'tables') such as the *Poulnabrone Dolmen*. In the village of Kilfenora, the *Burren Centre* of-

The vertical Cliffs of Moher get steeper as they jut out of the Atlantic

BURREN ★ (132 C5) (*M D12*)

Stretching out across the northwest of County Clare, the Burren, an area of some 160 km²/61 sq mi of bare limestone, appears like a lunar landscape. Arctic and alpine plants grow next to each other; in summer even orchids flower here *(www.burrenbeo.com)*.

Right in the heart of the Burren, ● *Aillwee Cave (daily 10am–6pm | admission 12 euros | 5 km/3 mi south of Bally-vaughan | www.aillweecave.ie)* is an un-

fers a permanent exhibition and an audiovisual presentation. A good option for accommodation is The Burren Hostel *(124 beds | Kincora Road | Lisdoon-varna | tel. 065 7074036 | www.sleep zone.ie | Budget)*.

Yoga classes can be booked at the proactive ● *Burren Yoga Centre (Lig do Scith | Normangrove | Cappaghmore | near Kinvara | tel. 091/637680 | www. burrenyoga.com)*. Yoga teachers from abroad often come here to teach.

The Twelve Pins mountain range crowns the rugged landscape of Connemara

CLIFFS OF MOHER
⭐ (132 B5) (*m C13*)

Stretching over 8 km/5 mi, the Unesco-listed Cliffs of Moher reach heights of up to 214 m/702 ft. There are many sections where they just near-vertically out of the Atlantic. The *Cliffs of Moher Visitor Centre (Nov–Feb 9am–5pm, March/April/Sept/Oct 9am–6pm, May/June 9am–7pm, July–Aug 9am–9pm | admission 6 euros | www.cliffsofmoher.ie)* presents an excellent exhibition. In good weather, climb ⚡ *O'Brien's Tower (admission 2 euros)* for views all the way to the Aran Islands. The Cliffs of Moher provide a habitat for huge colonies of birds. A one-hour INSIDERTIP boat tour with *Doolin 2 Aran Ferries (March–Oct daily 12pm, 3pm, 5pm | 15 euros | from Hafen Doolin | tel. 065 7075949 | www.cliffs-of-mohercruises.com)* allows you to view the cliffs from the water, together with their abundant seabird life.

CONNEMARA ⭐
(132 B 2–3) (*m C10–11*)

Founded in 1812, the town of *Clifden* (pop. 1500) is the starting point for a biking tour of some 150 km/93 mi across the coastal route through Connemara, truly beautiful in parts, and for a visit to the mountain range of *The Twelve Pins* to the east. The barren landscape has a charm all of its own; low stone walls crisscross the fields, and the coastline itself is lined by beautifully white sandy beaches. Old country traditions live on in Connemara, and Irish is still spoken here too. On the N 59, between Recess and Letterfrack, you will find *Kylemore Abbey & Garden (April–Sept 9am–6pm, Oct–March 10am–4pm | admission 13 euros | www.kylemoreabbey.tourism.ie)*. Today, the beautiful 19th-century neo-Gothic fairytale castle is run as an Education Centre by a Benedictine order. Four rooms of the abbey, surrounded by green hills and lakes, as well as the Gothic church and the gardens are open to the public. In an old Franciscan monastery in *Roundstone*, Malachy Kearns, the only Irishman who still makes bodhrán drums in the traditional way by hand, shows how the popular Irish folk music instrument is born, in his workshop INSIDER TIP. *Roundstone Music and Crafts (The Monastery | in summer daily, in winter Mon–Sat 9am–7pm | www.bodhran.com*

WESTPORT

(132 B1) *(C10)* **The drive through Connemara leads to Westport on Clew Bay, a bay sprinkled with numerous small islands.**

The small town (pop. 3500), a Georgian gem, snuggles around an octagonal square and is divided by the channelled narrow Carrowbeg River. Founded in the 18th century, the town owed its prosperity to the trade in yarns and fabrics, and its port. In the 19th century, it lost out to the English textile industry and the building of a railway line from Dublin. Today, tourism is blossoming.

SIGHTSEEING

OLD HARBOUR

Warehouses and quay infrastructure from Westport's founding days reflect the town's former economic heyday. *The Quay*

GEORGIAN RESIDENCES

Houses from the 18th and 19th centuries with well-preserved frontages line the main street, *The Mall*. The prettiest, with an impressive entrance portal, stands at the neo-Romanesque *St Mary's church*, which is also worth seeing.

WESTPORT HOUSE

Standing among the ruins of an old pirate's castle is a massive Gregorian manor. Pirate queen Grace O'Malley had it built for her great-granddaughter Maude in the 17th century. One of the most magnificent houses of Ireland, it's now filled with art and memories left by the generations of inhabitants. One of the castle's kitchens has now become *The Old Kitchen Café* where they serve apple pie fresh from the oven! Children love the carousels and boats at the adjoining *Pirate Adventure Park*. *Enter from The Quay | Jun–Aug daily 10am–6pm, March–May, Sept / Oct. 10am–4pm | admission 13 euros, plus Pirate Adventure Park 21 euros | www.westporthouse.ie*

LOW BUDGET

No charge: the very well-preserved 15th-century town palace of *Lynch's Castle (Shop Street | Galway)*, which is now a bank, may be visited for free.

The *Clew Bay Heritage Centre (April/May/Oct Mon–Fri 10am–2pm, June–Sept 10am–3pm, July/Aug also Sun 3–5pm | admission 3 euros | The Quay | www.westportheritage.com)* in Westport presents objects, documents and photos about the history of Clew Bay.

The *Old Mill Holiday Hostel (52 beds | Barrack Yard | James Street | tel. 098 2 70 45 | www.oldmillhostel.com)*, a pretty 18th-century quarrystone building in the heart of Westport, also offers good-value double rooms.

FOOD & DRINK

CRONIN'S SHEEBEEN

A thatched house on Clew Bay. This restaurant is a place of pilgrimage for fans of fancy fish dishes (such as seafood chowder or lobster). Meet with others for a Guinness and bar food snacks in the pub. *Daily noon–2.30pm and 6.30–10pm | Rosberg | tel. 098 2 6528 | www.croninssheebeen.com | Expensive*

THE IDLE WALL

A nautical rustic atmosphere pervades this restaurant in a historical cottage on Westport's harbour – a popular place to enjoy oysters and fish dishes. *Tue–Sat 5.30pm–10pm | The Quay | at the entrance to Westport House | tel. 098 5 06 92 | www.theidlewall.ie | Moderate*

INSIDER TIP THE TOWERS BAR & RESTAURANT

Seafood chowder and a Guinness: Modern, comfortably furnished bistro restaurant with pub and a spacious garden. A handful of guest rooms are available. Splendid view of the Croagh Patrick. *Mon–Thu, Sun 12.30pm–11.30pm, Fr/Sat 12.30pm–12.30am | The Quay | tel. 098 2 48 44 | www.thetowersbar.com | Moderate*

ENTERTAINMENT

INSIDER TIP MATT MOLLOY'S

There's traditional music on a daily basis in the pub owned by Matt Molloy, who plays the flute with the famous Irish folk band The Chieftains. *Bridge Street | www.mattmolloy.com*

WHERE TO STAY

ARDMORE COUNTRY HOUSE

Small, well-run hotel with a cosy atmosphere. The ✵ restaurant affords pretty views of the hills and Clew Bay. *13 rooms | The Quay | tel. 098 25 994 | www.ardmorecountryhouse.com | Moderate*

WESTPORT COAST HOTEL

Most ✵ rooms boast fabulous views of the harbour. All creature comforts, swimming pool, spa, a fine restaurant. *85 rooms | The Quay | tel. 098 2 90 00 | www.westportcoasthotel.ie | Expensive*

THE WYATT

Older, typically Irish hotel with a bright yellow frontage and view of Westport's central square. Often live music in the bar. *52 rooms | The Octagon | tel. 098 2 50 27 | www.wyatthotel.com | Budget*

INFORMATION

TOURIST INFORMATION OFFICE

Bridge Street | tel. 098 2 57 11 | www.westporttourism.com

WHERE TO GO

ACHILL ISLAND (132 A1) (∅ B9)

The country's largest island is connected to the mainland by a swing bridge since 1888. On Atlantic Drive, the stretch between Cloughmore and Dooega offers up magnificent views of a harsh nature with bog and heather landscapes, spectacular cliffs and beautiful sandy beaches. It was on this island – some 19 km/12 mi long and 22 km/13.5 mi wide – that German Nobel Prize-winning author Heinrich Böll wrote his 'Irish Journal'. Böll's former residence in Dugort, *Heinrich Böll Cottage (www.heinrichboellcottage.com)* is used today by international artists who have been given a scholarship to stay here some weeks. While the island, with a population of under 3000, can seem fairly desolate in winter, in summer the few guesthouses and hotels fill up quickly. Visitors keen on staying at Keel Bay in the west near Achill Head (a narrow cove with charming sandy beaches), should book ahead. The island's water sports centre is particularly popular with windsurfers. *www.achilltourism.com*

CROAGH PATRICK ☀

(132 B2) (𝄞 C10)

It's best to start at *Murrisk Abbey* to climb this 765 m/2500 ft-high conical mountain (89 km/55 mi southwest of Westport). The starting point is an Augustinian friary on the bay, dating back to 1457. The small chapel on the summit yields fabulous panoramic views all the way to Achill Island. It is said that in the year 441 St Patrick fasted up here for 40 days. Since then the mountain has been a pilgrimage destination for the Irish, particularly on the last Sunday in July. Legend tells how Patrick rang his bell to attract all the snakes in Ireland, who fell to their death into the abyss, thus freeing the country from snakes for all times. From *Murrisk*, with a statue of St Patrick slightly above the friary, it will take you about two hours to ascend to the summit. The *Croagh Patrick Visitor Centre (www.croagh-patrick.com)* is open between April and Oct, offering crafts and a restaurant alongside information.

NEWPORT

(132 B1) (𝄞 C9)

The road leads north along Clew Bay to Newport (13 km/8 mi). The route is manageable by bike, being the only one around Westport not involving hills. Look out for a 19th-century railway bridge that was part of a former railway service from Achill Island via Newport to Westport with onwards connection to Dublin. And don't miss *Carrickhowley Castle 5 km/3 mi* outside Newport. The tower house dating back to the 16th century with round corner towers used to belong to the Pirate Queen Grace O'Malley (1530–1603). In Ireland, numerous ballads keep alive the memory of this daughter of a clan chief and worthy adversary of Queen Elizabeth I.

Croagh Patrick: Pilgrimage walkers following in the footsteps of Saint Patrick

THE NORTHWEST

Donegal and Sligo, the two northern-most counties in Ireland, are dominated by mountainous landscapes, fine sandy beaches, numerous lakes and jagged coastlines.

Even though the sun often plays hard-to-get here, Donegal and Sligo have a charm all on their own. The landscape is isolated and wild and has a touch of melancholy. Wherever you go you will encounter testimonies to the past, such as the remains of a prehistoric cult of the dead at the tombs of *Carrowmore* – probably the oldest prehistoric burial places in Ireland – and Bronze Age stone circles.

In west Donegal, Gaelic customs and language are still widespread. People still earn their living traditionally in agriculture or in the tweed mills. However,

more resources are being made available for tourism, and there is now a direct flight from Dublin to Carrickfinn in the west of Donegal.

SLIGO

(129 E5) (ⵍ E8) The small port of Sligo (pop. 20,000) on the estuary of the Garavogue River in Sligo Bay lies at the heart of Ireland's northwest.

County Sligo, a region full of mountains, lakes, forests and rivers, was home to the poet W. B. Yeats. The Nobel Prize winner called it *The Land of Heart's Desire* and immortalised the mythic beauties of the region in the drama of that name as a literary monument.

Photo: Dolmen in Carrowmore

From Sligo to Donegal: The Gaelic language, its traditions, prehistoric tombs, wild landscapes and a touch of melancholy

Everywhere you go in town, buildings and inscriptions commemorate the poet who grew up in Sligo. The annual *Yeats International Summer School* in August attracts over 200 students and professors from all over the world. This place of Yeatsian pilgrimage offers devotees inspiring seminars, lectures, walks and evening chats in the pubs. Another site of pilgrimage for numerous Yeats fans is the island of *Innisfree* south of Sligo in Lough Gill, immortalised in a Yeats poem.

In summer, Sligo wakes up from its pro-

vincial slumber; the streets fill with people strolling, pubs and shops remain open until late at night. Rising temperatures bring about a near-Mediterranean atmosphere. It's worth scheduling a stopover in Sligo if only for the substantial number of cosy pubs. One of the most beautiful has been around for 150 years: INSIDER TIP *Hargadon's (4/5 O'Connell Street | tel. 071 915 37 09 | www.harga dons.com)* is a gem with flagstone floors, traditional turf fire and separate wood-panelled booths. Sligo is also a popular starting point for tours of several days into Donegal, Ireland's northernmost county.

The other focal point is William Butler Yeats. The art gallery shows Expressionistic landscape paintings by his younger

Sligo: The town of little pleasures and a many cosy pubs

SIGHTSEEING

SLIGO ABBEY

Over the course of the centuries, the 13th-century Dominican monastery suffered severe damage several times. The ruins still have a strong atmosphere. There is a cloister, and tombstones from the Gothic and Renaissance periods lie on a meadow. Look out for the fine stonemasonry work on a 15th-century high altar. *April–Oct daily 10am–6pm | admission 5 euros | Abbey Street*

SLIGO COUNTY MUSEUM ★

Millennia-old dolmens (burial sites constructed from stone blocks) and mystic stone circles are presented in a quantity unrivalled elsewhere in the British Isles.

brother Jack Butler Yeats, who was one of Ireland's most important 20th-century artists. *May–Sept Tue–Sat 9.30am–12.30pm and 2–5pm, Oct–April Tue–Sat 9.30am–12.30pm | admission free | Stephen Street*

YEATS MEMORIAL BUILDING

William Butler Yeats, poet, dramatist and critic, was born on 13 June 1865 in Dublin and grew up in Sligo. Yeats is one of the most-anthologised lyricists of modern times, receiving the Nobel Prize for Literature in 1923. For a long while Yeats lived in this pretty building, erected by his grandfather. *Tue–Sun 10am–5pm | free admission | O'Connell Street/ Wine Street | Hyde Bridge | www.yeats society.com*

FOOD & DRINK

AUSTIES RESTAURANT & BAR
Fish specialities, seafood from the Atlantic and traditional Irish lamb dishes. Vegetarians are catered for, too. *Mon–Sat 3pm–9pm, Sun 12.30pm–8.30pm | Rosses Upper | Rosses Point | tel. 071 9 11 77 86 | www.austies.ie | Moderate*

BISTRO BIANCONI
For many, this is the best Italian restaurant in Ireland: crispy pizzas, lasagne and various pasta dishes. On a budget? Go for the *Early Bird Dinner* in the afternoon. Very popular, especially at the weekend. *Daily from 5pm | Tobergal Lane | tel. 071 9 14 17 44 | www.bistro bianconi.ie | Moderate*

FIDDLERS CREEK
This welcoming cross between a pub and rustic restaurant serves inexpensive classics such as chicken wings or garlic mushrooms in the bar, then for dinner tortilla, steaks or exotically refined specialities such as salmon in a ginger-lime sauce. *Daily noon–4pm and from 5pm | Rockwood Parade | tel. 071 9 14 18 66 | www. fiddlerscreek.ie | Budget*

SHOPPING

MICHAEL KENNEDY CERAMICS
Vases, candlesticks, bowls, most of them in a strong purple colour – the artist is known all over the country for his designs inspired by Irish nature. *6 Market Street | Market Cross*

MICHAEL QUIRKE
As his handwritten business card reveals, the Wood Carver and Story Teller brings Irish mythology to life in his woodcarvings. Michael warmly welcomes any visitors who are interested in his work. *Tue–Sat 10.30am–1pm and 3–5pm | Wine Street*

LEISURE & SPORTS

INSIDER TIP EAGLES FLYING
Amazing to watch as white-tailed eagles and other birds of prey soar high into the sky and then return to the falconer. You can also take a tour of the enclosures beforehand. *April–Oct 10.30am–12.30pm and 2.30pm–4.30pm, Bird Show (1 hr) 11am and 3pm | admission 11.90 euros | 20 km/ 12 mi south of Sligo, between N 17 and Ballymote | www.eaglesflying.com*

KILCULLEN'S SEAWEED BATHS
Once people bathed in seawater and seaweed in order to combat rheumatism and arthritis, today to fight stress or cellulite. *Mon–Fri 12pm–8pm, Sat/Sun 10am–8pm, Jun-Aug daily 10am–9pm | 25 euros / bath (1.5–2 hrs) | Pier Road | Inishcrone (Enniscrone) | tel. 096 3 62 38 | www.kilcullenseaweedbaths.net*

⭐ **Sligo County Museum**
A fascinating presentation of the life and times of William Butler Yeats → **p. 82**

⭐ **Carrowmore**
A megalithic cemetery and the grave of a queen → **p. 85**

⭐ **Giant's Causeway**
It is said that a giant carried thousands of hexagonal basalt columns – for love → **p. 86**

⭐ **Lough Derg**
The charming inland lake is an all-year-round bird sanctuary → **p. 87**

MARCO POLO HIGHLIGHTS

ROSSES POINT (129 E5) (*m E8*)

The *County Sligo Golf Club (tel. 071 9 17 71 34 | www.countysligogolfclub. ie)* is situated approx. 7 km/4.3 mi northwest of Sligo in the district Rosses Point and is for many Ireland's most stunning golf course. Sun worshippers can't get enough of the long sandy beaches and small beach bars, and it's a meeting place for deep-sea anglers and windsurfers. *Details from the tourist information*

SLIGO RIDING CENTRE

The riding centre (4 km/2.5 mi away) offers beach rides or trail rides into the nearby hills and forests. Tuition takes place in a large covered arena and an outside paddock. You can choose to stay longer, for a package with accommodation, hacks and tuition. *Carrowmore | tel. 087 2 30 48 28 | www.sligoridingcentre.com*

VOYA SEAWEED BATHS ●

Taking a bath in seaweed used to be an Irish tradition – at the beginning of the 20th century, there were still hundreds of bath houses. Today, detoxifying seaweed baths are back in fashion. Massages and full-body wraps are on offer too – in an attractive luxurious ambience. *Daily 10am–8pm | 28 euros/50 min | Strand hill | tel. 071 9 16 86 86 | www.voyasea weedbaths.com*

HAWK'S WELL THEATRE

This small theatre puts on mainly Irish plays. *Temple Street | tel. 071 9 16 15 18 | www.hawkswell.com*

INSIDER TIP ▶ SHEELA-NA-GIG (FUREY'S)

Typically Irish pub, popular with the locals. Three to four times a week traditional live music, Wednesdays jazz evening. *Bridge Street*

WHERE TO STAY

SLIGO CITY HOTEL

The redbrick building with clocktower and granite portico offers well-kept rooms in a top central location, as well as a restaurant and pub. *60 rooms | Quay Street | tel. 071 9 14 40 00 | www.sligocity hotel.com | Budget*

SLIGO GREAT SOUTHERN HOTEL

The elegant façade hides large rooms, a high level of comfort – and *Finnegan's Bar. 98 rooms | Strandhill Road | tel. 071 9 16 21 01 | www.greatsouthernhotelsligo. ie | Expensive*

INSIDER TIP ▶ TEMPLE HOUSE

Extensive country estate amidst pastures and forests. The guest rooms are furnished with antique furniture. The many activities on offer include horse riding and fishing. *6 rooms | April–Nov | Ballymote | a good 19 km/12 mi south of Sligo | tel. 071 9 18 33 29 | www.templehouse.ie | Moderate*

INFORMATION

TOURIST OFFICE

Bank Building | O'Connell Street | tel. 071 9 16 12 01 | www.sligotourism.ie

WHERE TO GO

BALLYSHANNON (129 E4) (*m F7*)

The pretty little town (pop. 2800) on the estuary of the River Erne is the birthplace of the late musician Rory Gallagher, who was born here in 1948 at the Rock (!) Hospital and became one of the best guitarists on the European music scene of the 1970s. To commemorate the blues-rock legend who died in 1995, many bands find their way to Ballyshannon *(early June | www.rorygallagherfestival.com)*

for the INSIDER TIP ▶ *Rory Gallagher International Tribute Festival*. Visitors preferring a less rocky visit appreciate the two potteries of national fame, as well as pretty craft shops. It's also worth timing your visit to coincide with the *Ballyshannon Folk & Traditional Music Festival (first weekend of August | www.ballyshannonfolkfestival.com)*, a showcase of traditional Irish music, attracting well-known performers as well as newcomers.

BUNDORAN (129 E4) *(㎡ F7)*

Taking the N 15 in the direction of Donegal takes you past Drumcliffe, the site of W. B. Yeats' grave, to the sea resort of Bundoran (pop. 1800). The sandy beaches are good for water sports of all kinds, while golfers too enjoy coming here. Adults can take surf lessons or join a fishing trip, children will enjoy the leisure pool complex. Accommodation with sea view in the traditional *Fitzgerald's Hotel (16 rooms | Main Road | tel. 071 9 84 13 36 | www.fitzgeraldshotel.com | Moderate)*.

CARROWMORE ★
(129 E5) *(㎡ E8)*

Carrowmore (4 km/2.5 mi southwest of Sligo) boasts the second-largest megalithic cemetery in Europe. The complex was set up in approx. 3850 BC, long before the Celts came to Ireland, and is even older than Newgrange! Stroll amongst the remains of dolmens, stone circles and burial chambers of Carrowkeel, and climb the nearby mountain of *Knocknarea* (there is a signposted *Chambered Cairn* trail from Sligo)! The cairn on top of the ☼ summit is said to be the last resting place of Queen Maeve. Tradition has it that the belligerent Maeve – a central figure of Irish mythology – was buried standing up and in full armour. *April–Oct daily 10am–6pm | admission 5 euros*

DONEGAL (129 F3) *(㎡ F7)*

Donegal (pop. 2300) is a picturesque, provincial little town and a point of departure for ferries. It's surrounded by a landscape characterized by steep coasts and rugged spits of land. The town is located 65 km/40 mi northeast of the county town of Sligo and at the mouth of the River Eske in Donegal Bay. The centre is called *The Diamond*, a large pedestrian

Donegal Castle towers above the nearby market square and river

area flanked by a variety of lively cafés and tasteful hotels. The main square is the starting point for a sign-posted *walking tour*, leading past various sights, including *Donegal Castle (Easter–mid-Sept daily 10am–6pm, mid-Sept–Easter Thu–Mon 9.30am–4.30pm | admission 5 euros)*. On a self-guided tour you'll learn the history of an impressive residential

The former Ireland: The village of Glencolumbkille has many historical cottages

tower and the 17th-century manor. For accommodation with excellent an restaurant, look no further than the *Central Hotel (112 rooms | tel. 074 9 72 10 27 | www.centralhoteldonegal.com | Moderate)* with a pretty view of the square, the river and the bay. *Tourist information in Quay Street | tel. 074 9 72 11 48 | www. govisitdonegal.com*

GIANT'S CAUSEWAY ★
(130–131 C–D 1) *(ΩΩ J5)*

From Donegal, a drive of almost 145 km/90 mi via Londonderry/Derry leads to Northern Ireland's main attraction: over 38,000 hexagonal basalt columns jutting out of the wind-whipped ocean. Numerous myths surround the creation of the basalt columns. The most beautiful story tells how giant Finn MacCool fell madly in love with a young girl who lived on a remote island in the Hebrides. In order to get to his beloved with-

out getting his feet wet, Finn created this stony path. Scientists reckon that the Giant's Causeway was formed over 60 million years ago, when lava breaking through the earth's crust solidified.

Starting point for a hike along the natural formation, almost 3.2 km/2 mi north of Bushmills, is *Portballintrae*. From the *Visitor Centre (daily 9am–7pm | admission 9 euros)* a path leads to the coast (15 min). Before turning right for the Causeway, look out for *Camel Rock* jutting out of the water in Portnaboe Bay. A bit further on, you'll see the *Wishing Chair* which looks like a stone chair. At the *Organ* the near-vertical basalt columns jut up into the skies up to 15 m. From here, the steps of the *Shepherd's Path* lead onto the cliffs of the *Aird Snout* mountain. Nearby *Bushmills* is well worth a detour – this famous whiskey distillery *(March–Oct Mon–Sat 9am–5pm, Sun 12pm–5pm, Nov–Feb Mon–Sat 10am–5pm, Sun 12pm–5pm |*

admission 8 euros | www.bushmills.com) is the world's oldest.

GLENCOLUMBKILLE (129 D3) (*⊞ E7*)

At the end of a lonely mountain valley lies the village of Glencolumbkille (56 km/35 mi west of Donegal). At the *Folk Village Museum (Easter–Sept Mon–Sat 10am–6pm, Sun noon–6pm | admission 4.50 euros | www.glenfolkvillage. com)*, tours lead through cottages built between the 1700 to 1900. A school, a pub, a craft shop as well as a teashop complete the historical village. On the way back, it's well worth detouring to *Slieve League*, at 1968 ft the highest sea cliffs in Europe.

LOUGH DERG ★ (129 F3–4) (*⊞ F7*)

Mystic sites of faith: several islets lie at the centre of Lough Derg, an elongated lake surrounded by small villages, about 14.5 km/9 mi southeast of Donegal. Holy Island was the site of a 7th-century monastic settlement that is shrouded in myth (in the summer months, boat trips across can be organised from the harbour). Discover Early Christian tombstones, hermitage cells and four archaic chapels. For over a thousand years, *Station Island* has been a European site of pilgrimage. According to legend, St Patrick spent 40 days here praying and fasting. During the pilgrimage season between June and August, the island may only be visited by believers. These stay three days and three nights, their only sustenance black tea and toast. One-day (silent) retreats are also on offer; even families are given the opportunity for some inner contemplation. *www.loughderg.org*

LOUGH GILL (129 E5) (*⊞ E–F8*)

From Sligo, a 35-km/22-mi drive leads around Lough Gill, a picturesque lake amidst wooded hills. Leaving Sligo on the N 16, turn right onto the R 286, following signs to *Hazelwood Estate*. A side road brings you to *Half Moon Bay* (picnic site), the starting point for hikes along the lake and through the adjoining woods. Back on the R 286, you reach *Parke's Castle (April–Sept daily 10am–6pm | admission 5 euros)*, a 17th-century fort. At the entrance to the village of Dromahair, a path leads to the Franciscan monastery of *Creevylea Abbey* of 1508. The path following on from there leads away from the lake, only joining up with it again at *Dooney Rock Forest*. An information brochure on the beautiful nature trail along the lake shore can be picked up at the car park.

STRANDHILL (129 E5) (*⊞ E8*)

This popular holiday village lies on the coast (approx. 8 km/5 mi west of Sligo). Swimming can be dangerous here: look out for lifeguards and flags. Sligo's airport is also near Strandhill, offering sightseeing flights with light aircraft alongside services to Dublin.

LOW BUDGET

Inexpensive accommodation at the *Harbour House (48 beds | Finisklin Road | Sligo | tel. 071 9 17 15 47 | www. harbourhousehostel.com)*: the hostel, once the residence of the harbourmaster, is only 10 minutes walk into the town centre and the bus/train station.

If being in Strandhill suddenly makes you want to ride some waves, you'll find used surfboards at *Perfect Day (Shore Road | Strandhill | Sligo | tel. 087 2 02 93 99 | www.perfectday surfing.ie*

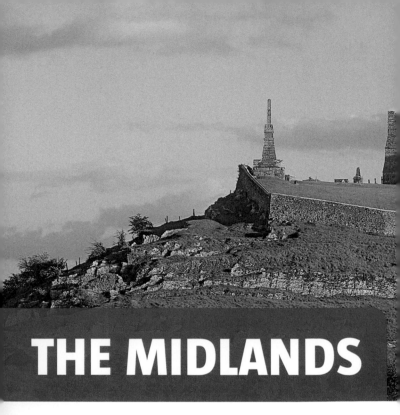

THE MIDLANDS

Rainbows arching over gentle hills, wide plains as far as the eyes can see and loads of friendly villages. Welcome to Ireland's heartland. Between Dublin and Galway, it's covered with small lakes and reminders of the Christian culture which is so significant in Ireland.

The typical Irish landscape – sleepy little towns with a legendary history placed between lush green fields and rocky hills. There is also a medieval gem just waiting to be discovered in the Midlands: Kilkenny will conquer any visitor's heart.

KILKENNY

(139 D2) (∅ H14) This Irish city looks great on a postcard. Kilkenny (pop. 26,000) is the best-preserved medieval city in Ireland. It's also the best place to go if you're looking for handmade art. The artists here offer a ton of handicafts and the streets boast an eclectic array of studios and shops.

Colourful façades and centuries-old pubs. Winding alleyways, traditional shops and the splendid complex of Kilkenny Castle on the River Nore. This landmark is what gives the city its unique charm. Kilkenny is also the capital of County Kilkenny. In the Middle Ages, the city was even the unofficial capital of Ireland and had its own Anglo-Norman parliament. The urban and cultural heritage of that era, as well as the idyllic surroundings, are best explored by bike. There's also a lot of rustic-looking pubs to discover here.

Photo: Rock of Cashel with cathedral

The cradle of Christianity. Here you'll find a number of ruins revealing the history of the region's many monasteries

SIGHTSEEING

BLACK ABBEY

In the carefully restored abbey, a Dominican church founded around 1225, Holy Mass is still said on a daily basis. The lead-glazed rosary window consisting of five vertical segments is an impressive sight to see. Known as the 'Rosary Window', it's particularly beautiful when the sun shines through it. Small donations are very much appreciated here. *Daily 8am–6pm | Abbey Street*

CATHEDRAL CHURCH OF ST CANICE

This 13th-century medieval cathedral has become a stone symbol of faith. Among its treasures are age-old tombs of wealthy citizens who lived before 1280. A steep set of stairs lead you the cathedral's ☀️ round tower 30 m/98 ft above ground. *April, May, Sept Mon–Sat 10am–1pm, 2pm–5pm, Sun 1pm–6pm, Oct–March Mon–Sat 10am–1pm and 2pm–4pm, Sun 2pm–4pm | admission 4 euros | Coach Road | www.stcanices cathedral.com*

INSIDER TIP **CULTURE TRAIL**

This cultural trail through Kilkenny's streets takes you to places of interest, pubs and restaurants, arts and crafts shops, to the local market and the theatre (brochure available from the tourist information centre).

KILKENNY CASTLE ⭐

Built in 1190, the Norman fortification served as the family seat of the influential Butler family until 1967. Charging the symbolic sum of 50 pounds, Arthur But-

ROTHE HOUSE

Kilkenny's regional museum is housed in three burghers' houses in the Tudor style. These buildings, erected between 1594 and 1610, alone are worth a visit. 18th-century paintings, antique furniture and historic exhibits from the region are presented in the white-washed rooms with pretty oak-beam ceilings. An insider tip for garden lovers is the adjoining *Rothe Garden*, laid out in 17th-century style, in which kitchen herbs,

Kilkenny: Medieval gem with pubs in winding streets

ler gave the crumbling castle to the Irish state, which started a comprehensive restoration programme. Today, Kilkenny's landmark is resplendent again, presenting numerous attractions. A 45-minute guided tour shows antique furniture as well as oil paintings of the Butler clan. The lower floor houses the *Butler Gallery (admission free | www.butlergallery.com)*, one of Ireland's foremost galleries for contemporary art. *April–Sept 9.30am–5.30pm, Oct–March 9.30am–4.30pm | admission 8 euros | The Parade | www.kilkennycastle.ie*

fruit trees and flowers from traditional peasant gardens thrive. *Mon–Sat 10.30am–5pm, Sun 12pm–5pm | admission 5.50 euros | Parliament Street | www.rothehouse.com*

SHEE ALMS HOUSE

The Tudor house built in 1582 by Sir Richard Shee houses the *Tourist Information Centre*. Here, the prosperous Shee merchant family accommodated old, sick and poor citizens: the almshouse performed its charitable duty up until 1830. *Rose Inn Street*

FOOD & DRINK

ANOCHT
Coffee shop and restaurant in the Kilkenny Design Centre across from Kilkenny Castle. Delicious snacks. *Thu–Sat from 5pm | Castle Yard | tel. 056 7 72 21 18 | www.kilkennydesign.com | Moderate*

CAFÉ SOL
Fresh ingredients, friendly service: café-restaurant opposite the Tholsel (town hall) serving Irish-Mediterranean fare. *Mon–Thu 11am–9.30pm, Fri/Sat 11am–10pm, Sun noon–9pm | 6 William Street | tel. 056 7 76 49 87 | www.cafesolkilkenny. com | Moderate*

INSIDER TIP FOODWORKS CAFÉ
Gnocchi and fish and chips – well prepared, nice atmosphere. *Daily 12pm–2.30pm, Thu–Sat 5pm–10pm | 7 Parliament Street | tel. 056 7 77 76 96 | www. foodworks.ie | Moderate*

RISTORANTE RINUCCINI
An Irish-Italian couple combining refined with rustic cuisine – unsurpassable. *Daily noon–3pm and 5pm–10pm | 1 The Parade | opposite the Castle | tel. 056 7 76 15 75 | www.rinuccini.com | Moderate*

SHOPPING

KILKENNY DESIGN CENTRE ★
The artists in their workshops in the former mews of Kilkenny Castle are always developing new designs from materials such as ceramics, gold and silver, glass, wood and wool. Popular souvenirs, alongside fancy Barbour waxed garments, are woollen wares from Donegal of the *Fishermen out of Ireland brand*. The high prices are due to the goods' top quality. *Daily 10am–7pm | Castle Yard | off Castle Road | www.kilkennydesign.com*

ENTERTAINMENT

EDWARD LANGTON BAR & RESTAURANT
Stylish rustic atmosphere; the hotel bar has received the 'Pub of the Year' garland a few times already. *69 John Street | www.langtons.ie*

KYTELER'S INN
Pub with live entertainment: bar food (Irish fare) with live music every day. It is supposed to have been the home of Alice Kyteler in the 14th century: Accused of witchcraft, she fled the country only for a servant to be condemned to death instead. Pretty courtyard with two fountains. *Daily from noon | St Kieran's Street | tel. 056 7 72 10 64 | www. kytelersinn.ie*

★ **Kilkenny Castle**
Wonderfully preserved medieval stronghold → p. 90

★ **Kilkenny Design Centre**
Pioneer of Irish craft design → p. 91

★ **Carrick-on-Suir**
Pretty small town on the river Suir → p. 93

★ **Rock of Cashel**
The elevated plateau with the famous cathedral was the seat of kings and a site of St Patrick's miracle work → p. 93

★ **Dunmore Cave**
Imposing stalactite cave with many long corridors, where evidence was found of a Viking attack 1000 years ago → p. 94

MARCO POLO HIGHLIGHTS

The Great Telescope at Birr Castle: This large structure dates back to 1840 and still works!

WHERE TO STAY

BUTLER HOUSE

Hiding behind the façade, festooned with creepers, of the former residence of 18th-century Lady Eleanor Butler, puristically elegant and individually styled rooms and suites await. To partake of the exquisite breakfast, walk through the garden into the rooms of the former Kilkenny stables. *12 rooms | 16 Patrick Street | tel. 056 772 28 28 | www.butler.ie | Moderate*

GLENDINE INN

250-year-old pub, a 20-minute walk from the city centre, with en-suite rooms. *10 rooms | Castlecomer Road | tel. 056 772 10 69 | www.glendineinn.com | Budget*

KILKENNY RIVER COURT ☼

Four-star hotel with swimming pool, gym and a splendid view across the river to Kilkenny Castle. The large rooms are furnished in country style, the three-course lunch in the *Riverside Restaurant* is a local institution. Unsurpassed is afternoon tea in the sunshine on the terrace of the *Riverview Bar. 88 rooms | The Bridge | off John Street | tel. 056 772 33 88 | www.river courthotel.com | Expensive*

ZUNI

Chic and sophisticated. Kilkenny's first theatre from 1902 now houses an extraordinary boutique hotel. Equally renowned is the in-house restaurant, island-wide known for Maria Raferty's modern Irish cuisine. *13 rooms | 26 Patrick Street | tel. 056 772 39 99 | www.zuni. ie | Moderate*

INFORMATION

TOURIST INFORMATION OFFICE

Shee Alms House | Rose Inn Street | tel. 056 775 15 00 | www.kilkennytourism.ie

WHERE TO GO

BIRR (138 A5) (*ᴫ F12*)

The small town of Birr (pop. 5000) lies 70 km/44 mi northwest of Kilkenny. Many are drawn here by its fabulous green spaces such as the *Millennium Gardens* (belonging to the Earls of Rosse) which is the country's largest. The castle (*daily 9am–6pm | admission 9 euros | www.birrcastle.com*) is also attractive and boasts a INSIDER TIP historic telescope. From 1840 onwards, the third Earl of Rosse built the world's largest telescope (which it was for 70 years, and, by the way, it still works!). His son was able to correctly determine the temperature of the moon. Accommodation options include *Doolys Hotel (18 rooms | Emmet Square | tel. 057 9 12 00 32 | www.doolyshotel.com | Moderate)*, a 250-year-old coach station on the town's Georgian central square, with a good restaurant.

CAHIR (138 B3) (*ꚰ F15*)

Erected in the 13th century in the pretty village of Cahir (70 km/44 mi southwest), situated on a small rocky island in the river Suir, the stronghold of Cahir Castle (*daily 9.30am–5.30pm | admission 5 euros*) was extended and remodelled several times up to the 19th century. Under the Earls of Ormond, the impregnable castle developed into one of the most powerful in the country. Wish to stay longer? Then best you check in at the *Cahir House Hotel (41 rooms | The Square | tel. 052 7 44 30 00 | www.cahirhousehotel.ie | Moderate)*.

In a stone house belonging to the old mill, the INSIDER TIP *Galileo Café (Church Street | Mill Building | tel. 052 7 44 56 89 | www.galileocafe.com | Budget–Moderate)* serves up Italian-Mediterranean fare; bring your own wine. Almost 3.2 km/2 mi southeast of town on a hill in Kilcommon southeast of town, discover *Swiss Cottage (daily 10am–6pm | admission 4 euros | access via Caher Wood and Ardfinnan Road, R 670)*, a splendid, thatched wooden house with 19th-century dormer windows.

CARRICK-ON-SUIR ★ (142 C3) (*ꚰ G15*)

This little town (pop. 6000, 40 km/25 mi south) is home of *Ormond Castle (March–Aug daily 10am–6pm | admission 5 euros)*, an Elizabethan-style, 16th-century structure with incredible architecture and decor. It stands on the banks of the River Suir. Take a short, entertaining tour and hear a number of inside stories, like the time the Queen was once expected for tea. TIP: Come on Friday when the local *Farmer's Market (10am–2pm | Heritage Center Grounds | Main Street)* takes place. Buy some delicacies and have a nice picnic. *www.carrickonsuirheritagecentre.com*

CASHEL (138 B3) (*ꚰ F14*)

The highlight in this little town (pop. 3200), a good 48 km/30 mi west on the N 8, is the imposing ★ *Rock of Cashel (daily, mid March–May 9am–5.30pm, June–mid-Sept 9am–7pm, mid-Sept–*

LOW BUDGET

The *Kilkenny Tourist Hostel (60 beds in 11 rooms | 35 Parliament Street | tel. 056 7 76 35 41 | www.kilkennyhostel.ie)*, a Georgian townhouse, offers good-value rooms.

Want to save the entrance fee for *Kilkenny Castle*? Take a free stroll through the park and visit the castle's in-house Butler Gallery of modern art *(www.butlergallery.com)*.

The *Brú Ború* arts centre *(June–Sept | tel. 062 6 11 22 | www.bruboru.ie)* at the foot of the Rock of Cashel puts on traditional music, folkdancing and readings; charges are either non-existent or low.

mid-March 9am–4.30pm | admission 8 euro). The Celts in their day already worshipped the rock, on which subsequently a cathedral (13th century), a chapel and a round tower were built. According to legend, it was here that St Patrick explained the Holy Trinity using a shamrock leaf – marking the birth of an Irish icon. The *Cashel Folk Village (mid-May–mid-June daily 9.30am–5.30pm, mid-Jun–mid-Sept daily 9am–7.30pm | admission 5 euros | www.cashelfolkvillage.ie)* on Dominic Street consists of reconstructions of thatched village shops and a chapel. At the *Cashel Heritage Centre (March–Oct daily 9.30am–5.30pm, Nov–Feb Mon–Fri 9.30am–5.30pm | admission free | City Hall | www.cashel.ie)* there's a model showing how the town looked in 1640. The INSIDER TIP *Cashel Palace Hotel (23 rooms | Main Street | tel. 062/627 07 | www.cashelpalace.ie | Expensive),* former residence of the archbishop, has been turned into a picture-postcard country house: marble fireplaces, oak parquet flooring and views of gardens or the Rock of Cashel. What a view! What a life!

CLONMACNOISE (134 A4) (ɷ F11)
Even on gloomy days, the ecclesiastical ruins, high crosses and the 19-m/62-ft round tower exude a powerful charm all their own. From the year 548 onwards, a community of monks found shelter in the abbey founded by the hermit Ciaran (Kieran). For nearly a millennium, the ecclesiastical and spiritual elite of the island lived in Clonmacnoise (119 km/74 mi northwest of Kilkenny on the River Shannon). Every year on 9 September, a pilgrimage takes place here. *Daily 10am–6pm | admission 8 euros*

DUNMORE CAVE ★ (138 D2) (ɷ H13)
Head just 12 km/7.5 mi north from towards *Castlecomer* on the N 78 to reach

FOR BOOKWORMS AND FILM BUFFS

Irish Journal – Thousands followed in the footsteps of Nobel-Prize winner Heinrich Böll to Achill Island off the west coast, where he had a holiday home

The Secret Scripture – Sebastian Barry's moving and unsentimental novel, told in two perspectives that join in a clever twist at the end

McCarthy's Bar – The late British TV comedian Pete McCarthy visits the country of his parents

Once – Independent film by John Carney (2007), a love story between a busker and an immigrant

Angela's Ashes – Frank McCourt's memory of life in the slums of Limerick won the Pulitzer Prize and was turned into a major film (2000) by Alan Parker

Ulysses – James Joyce reports the minutiae of a single day (16 June 1904) in the life of Dubliner Leopold Bloom

Round Ireland in Low Gear – Hilarious: British travel writer Eric Newby recounting his bike tours through the country

The Wind that shakes the Barley – film about the Irish fight for independence post-1916, winning Ken Loach the 2006 Palme d'Or

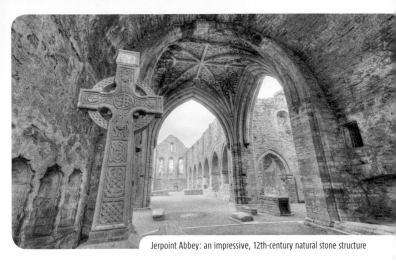

Jerpoint Abbey: an impressive, 12th-century natural stone structure

this massive limestone cave. Chosen in 928 as a place of refuge by people fleeing a Viking attack, this cave turned out to be a death trap as they were smoked out by their pursuers. During excavations in 1973, the remains of 44 people were discovered, mostly women and children. The cave is well-lit; just as well, with the steep descent into the widespread network of underground corridors. Down below cavities full of stalactites, stalagmites and columns await, amongst them the 7-m/23-ft *Market Cross,* Europe's largest free-standing stalagmite. *March–mid-June, mid-Sept–Oct daily 9.30am–5pm, mid-June–Sept daily 9.30am–6.30pm, Nov-Feb Wed-Sun 9.30am–5pm | admission 5 euros*

JERPOINT ABBEY (137 D3) *(𝄡 H14)*

Just esoterism? Nope. The ruins of this 12th-century Cistercian monastery (25 km/16 mi south) are radiating with secrets that even contemporaries will sense. Look closer! This castellated structure boasts a rectangular defensive tower and a 14th-century cloister decorated with sculptures. *March–Sept daily 9am–*

5.30pm, Oct/Nov 9am–4pm | admission 5 euros | Thomastown

SHANNON RIVER
(132–133 C–D6) *(𝄡 C–D14)*

The longest river in the country (nearly 402 km/250 mi) forms many large lakes between its Lough Allen source and the city of Limerick. It's great to take a houseboat or cabin cruiser on the river to the Grand Canal branching off towards Dublin. *www.river-shannon.com*

SLIEVE BLOOM MOUNTAINS
(134 B5) *(𝄡 G12)*

An ideal area for easy hikes (50 km/37 mi northwest of Kilkenny), such as the ✂ *Ard Erin*, only 609 m/1998 ft high. For a good 29 km/18 mi, the *Slieve Bloom Way* leads through forests and moorland. A good starting point is *Glen Barrow,* southwest of Rosenallis. A stylish choice of accommodation: *Roundwood House (10 rooms | tel. 057 8 73 21 20 | www.roundwoodhouse.com | Moderate)* near Mountrath, a country house – a mini 'Downton Abbey'.

DISCOVERY TOURS

1 IRELAND AT A GLANCE

START: **1** Dublin
END: **17** Sligo

10 days
Driving time
40 hours

Distance:
➡ approx. 1200 km/756 mi

COSTS: approx. 1400 euros (train, bus, accommodation, Ring of Kerry circular route, hire car, bicycle hire, admission, food)
WHAT TO PACK: swimwear, hiking shoes, rain jacket

IMPORTANT TIPS:
6 **Ring of Kerry:** book the circular route by bus in your hotel or travel agency beforehand!
11 **Cliffs of Moher:** car hire from e.g. **Enterprise Car Hire** *(Park Street | Limerick | www.enterprise.ie)*
14 **Connemara:** bicycle hire from **Bike Hire Ireland** *(Seamus Quirke Road | Galway | tel. 091 52 50 07 | www.bikeireland.com)*

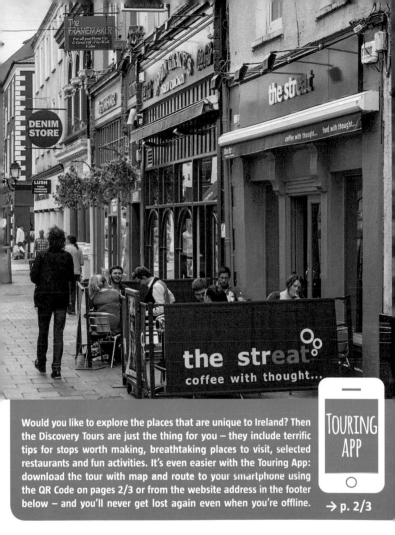

Would you like to explore the places that are unique to Ireland? Then the Discovery Tours are just the thing for you – they include terrific tips for stops worth making, breathtaking places to visit, selected restaurants and fun activities. It's even easier with the Touring App: download the tour with map and route to your smartphone using the QR Code on pages 2/3 or from the website address in the footer below – and you'll never get lost again even when you're offline.

TOURING APP

→ p. 2/3

Although this tour takes you to some of Ireland's most splendid landmarks, it also offers unusual insights into the country and its people.

The tour kicks off in **① Dublin** → p. 32. Discover the city centre by foot and take a **trip on the Liffey**: Ships from **Dublin Discovered Boat Tours** → p. 35 **harbour at Bachelors Walk.** Take a break sitting high above this vibrant and lively city's rooftops at the roof-terrace bar on the **Guinness Storehouse** → p. 35. Then visit the **Trinity College Library** → p. 39, to see the centuries old long room and the leg-

DAY 1

① Dublin

299 km/186 mi

Photo: Cork Street in Cork

97

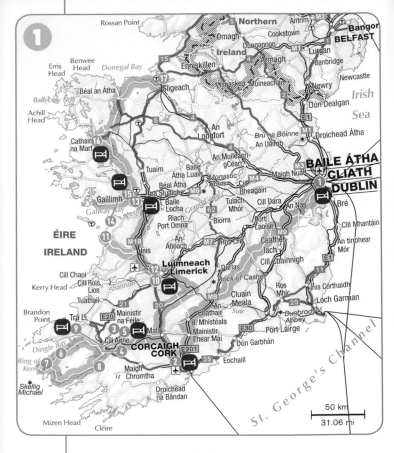

endary Book of Kells. At some point during the day meet up with half the city for a coffee and sandwich in **Bewley's Café** → p. 39. Definitely spend your evening in one of the pubs in the trendy district of **Temple Bar** → p. 38. and from there it's not far to the **Arlington Hotel** → p. 42 where you can spend the night.

DAY 2

2 Cork

🏙 🏛 ☕ 🛍 🏠 🚌

(102 km/63 mi)

In two to three hours by bus or train you're in **2** Cork → p. 46. Check out here the **Cork Butter Museum** → p. 48: dedicated to Irish butter: a down-to-earth, slightly bizarre, but most importantly: typically Irish experience. Then head to the splendid Victorian **market hall** where you can partake of a delicious cream tea at the **Farmgate**

Café → p. 50. Carry on **through the pedestrian zones past Georgian townhouses, cafes and shops and over the River Lee to the** **Shandon Church** → p. 50. Feel free to ring their bell!

The next day **the train takes you to the town of ❸ Killarney** → p. 58. After a stroll through the lively old town take **the city bus to the nearby ❹ Killarney National Park** → p. 59. After a guided tour through **Muckross House** → p. 58, a magnificent Victorian castle, enjoy lunch preferably outdoors in the **Muckross Garden Restaurant** → p. 60. Afterwards take **a walk through the park to Ross Castle** → p. 59 and let yourself be taken across the lake in a boat for just a couple of euros. Where to stay the night? Try the stylish **❺ Earls Court House** → p. 60 **situated between the town and national park.**

Your pre-booked **tour on the coastal and panoramic road of the ❻ Ring of Kerry** → p. 63 takes you around the Iveragh Peninsula, past mountains and deserted beaches with dramatic views of the majestic and raging Atlantic. In summer, the intrepid might want to brave the waves while also enjoying the sight of green pastures, stately homes and villages with brightly painted houses. A bridge leads to Valentia Island into the sleepy harbour town of **❼ Knightstown** → p. 63. Afterwards you might fancy stopping in the pretty town of **❽ Kenmare** → p. 63 for the catch of the day in a fish restaurant before returning to **❾ Killarney** → p. 58.

From Killarney, **the train takes you on the next day to ❿ Limerick** → p. 66 for a spot of art in the **Hunt Museum** → p. 67 before rewarding yourself with a warm apple pie with cream in the attached restaurant.

The next day, it's time for an **excursion to the famous ⓫ Cliffs of Moher** → p. 76: If you don't want to hire a rental car, take the bus or book a seat on an organised tour in Limerick. Back in **⓬ Limerick** we recommend an evening meal in **Freddy's Bistro** → p. 68, where an excellent Irish Guinness Stew is on the menu.

Hop on a bus again in Limerick to the vibrant university city of ⓭ Galway → p. 70. With its narrow lanes, second-hand bookshops full of wonderfull books and historic townhouses, the city is the perfect place to take

DAY 3

❸ Killarney

6.5 km/4 mi

❹ Killarney National Park

25 km/15.5 mi

❺ Earls Court House

42 km/26 mi

DAY 4

❻ Ring of Kerry

44 km/27 mi

❼ Knightstown

89 km/55 mi

❽ Kenmare

33 km/20.5 mi

❾ Killarney

162 km/101 mi

DAY 5

❿ Limerick

80 km/50 mi

DAY 6

⓫ Cliffs of Moher

80 km/50 mi

⓬ Limerick

101 km/63 mi

DAY 7

⓭ Galway

15 km/9.3 mi

a long stroll. After a portion of delicious fish 'n' chips at **McDonagh's Seafood House** → p. 73 plan your bike tour the next day over a Guinness at the **Róisín Dubh** → p. 73 After that, overnight accommodation is available at **Barnacle's Quay Street House** → p. 74.

The **bike tour** leads you through ⑭ **Connemara** → p. 76 along the **country road 336** and the Galway Bay coastline. It takes 18 km/11 mi to **An Spidéal** while **Casla** is another 20 km/12.5 mi away. You'll be spreading your towel on white unspoilt beaches. **Return to ⑮ Galway along the same road.**

The **bus ride from Galway to ⑯ Westport** → p. 77 **takes two hours**. After a stroll past Georgian townhouses and the market square, enjoy a meal **at the old harbour** at the **The Idle Wall** → p. 78 fish restaurant. Spend the afternoon in the manor house of **Westport House** → p. 77 and the evening in **Matt Molloy's Pub** → p. 78 listening to traditional Irish music.

Take the bus to ⑰ Sligo → p. 80, home to the great poet W. B. Yeats. A beer at **Hargadon's** → p. 81 is a must as well as a visit to the **Sligo County Museum** → p. 82 and **Yeats Memorial Building** → p. 82. And while you're here, think about stopping at the woodcarving workshop of **Michael Quirke** → p. 83 to complete your impressions of Ireland and its inhabitants.

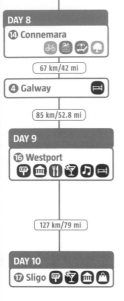

DAY 8

⑭ Connemara

🚴 🏊 ⛴ 🌳

67 km/42 mi

④ Galway 🛏

85 km/52.8 mi

DAY 9

⑯ Westport

🏙 🏛 🍴 🍸 🎵 🛏

127 km/79 mi

DAY 10

⑰ Sligo 🏙 🍸 🏛 🏨

② ON THE DINGLE WAY BETWEEN TRALEE AND DINGLE BAY

START: ❶ Tralee END: ❼ Dingle	3 days Walking time 6–7 hours a day
Distance: easy 🔄 59 km/37 mi ▫️▫️▫️ Altitude: 300 m/489 ft	

COSTS: approx. 300 euros/2 people (accommodation, food, return journey)

WHAT TO PACK: hiking gear, binoculars, rain jacket, snacks, water

IMPORTANT TIPS: The hiking trail is marked 'Dingle Way', more information is available at *www.dingleway.net*.

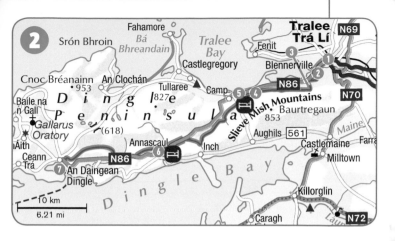

The 179 km/111 mi Dingle Way long-distance trail covers nearly the entire Dingle Peninsula. Particularly beautiful is the section between Tralee and Dingle leads you along mountain trails and through fern-covered valleys, along clear brooks, and offers repeated views across Tralee Bay and Dingle Bay.

From ❶ **Tralee** head in a **south-westerly** direction. For **2 km/1.2 mi the trail leads along the banks of the former Tralee Ship Canal** of 1846 towards the town of ❷ **Blennerville**. Today the canal is mostly silted up and harbouring swans and other waterfowl. Don't miss the old **sluice gates** at the harbour. This is where many Irish boarded the boat to America in the 19th century. A tourist attraction is the 200-year-old **windmill** *(June–Aug daily 9am–6pm, April/May and Sept/Oct daily 9.30am–5.30pm | admission 5 euros)*, beautifully restored and still working today – the largest in the British Isles. Grouped around the mill are an exhibition centre, craft shops and a restaurant. **From Blennerville, a quiet *country road* (single-lane, asphalted) leads southwards from the N 86 (after crossing the canal) gently ascending to ❸ Tonavane** on the slopes of the Slieve Mish Mountains. From Tonavane onwards the trail becomes more adventurous: **it heads westwards**, through boggy marshland stepping on old sandstone slabs. It runs over wooden bridges and stepping stones to cross brooks and over stiles through open mountain scenery with views of Tralee Bay; it is only just before ❹ **Killelton**, that the trail is paved again. In Killelton, a village abandoned in the 19th century, you can find the remnants of the **St Elton Oratory**. overgrown with ivy and fuchsia. The early Christian

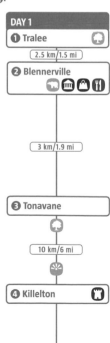

DAY 1

❶ Tralee

2.5 km/1.5 mi

❷ Blennerville

3 km/1.9 mi

❸ Tonavane

10 km/6 mi

❹ Killelton

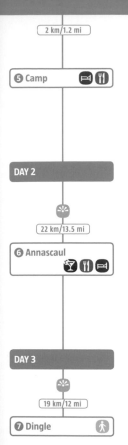

2 km/1.2 mi

⑤ Camp

oratory dates back to the 7th century. In the valley, **the trail crosses the Finglass River** and after 18 km/11 mi you have reached your destination for the first day (1 km/0.6 mi) off the Dingle Way): the village of **⑤ Camp (on the N 86),** where you can also stay overnight in the **Camp Junction House B&B** *(6 rooms | tel. 087 2 43 07 04 | www.camp-junctionhouse.com | Budget)*. The **Ashes Pub & Restaurant** *(daily | Camp Cross | tel. 066 713 01 33 | www.ashesbar.ie | Moderate)* serves good Irish food.

DAY 2

22 km/13.5 mi

⑥ Annascaul

Early next morning, **the Dingle Way carries on southwest across the Dingle Peninsul**a, taking you past extended boggy plains where peat is still cut. Towards the south the latter part of the day affords spectacular panoramic views towards Dingle Bay. On a clear day you can see the jagged mountain scenery of the neighbouring Iveragh Peninsula from here. You finally reach the small town of **⑥ Annascaul**. Over a dozen pubs are available for you to quench your thirst in the evening. The popular **South Pole Inn** *(daily | Main Street | tel. 066 915 73 88 | Budget)* is a good address for an evening meal. Afterwards, a recommended place to lay your head is **Teac Seáin** *(4 rooms | Main Street | tel. 066 915 70 01 | www.teacseain.com | Budget)*.

DAY 3

19 km/12 mi

⑦ Dingle

The stage goal for the third day is **Dingle**. However, before getting there, after a 20 km/12.5 mi hike and a 340 m/1115 ft ascent, enjoy the view of the historic Minard Castle in the distance, which occupies a splendid location above Kilmurry Bay. Carrying on through scattered villages finally takes you into lively **⑦ Dingle → p. 62** with its small port.

Hiking with spectacular views over the ruins of Minard Castle

3 BY BARGE FROM RATHANGÁN TO ST MULLINS

START: ❶ Rathangán
END: ❶ Rathangán

7 days
Driving time
50 hours

Distance:
↔ 200 km/124 mi

COSTS: 750–1300 euros for a boat, depending on season, plus food
WHAT TO PACK: swim wear, drinking water, food and snacks

IMPORTANT TIPS: narrowboats can be hired in Rathangán, 12 km/7.5 mi southwest from Robertstown from Canalways Ireland Barge Holidays → p. 124. No boating licence is needed as you are given a 40-minute induction before you start out especially on how to manoeuvre the barge through locks.

In the 19th century, the Grand Canal was a popular travel artery from Dublin to Shannon Harbour. This tour takes you on a barge from Rathangán to St Mullins. You gently sail through quiet nature, observing waterfowl, past overgrown stone bridges, historic locks and old villages.

From ❶ Rathangán, whose waters famously teem with a great variety of fish, **the River Barrow takes you to ❷ Monasterevin** with its historic drawbridge. For 150 years (until 1921), the town housed Cassidy's Distillery, a whiskey distillery, the historic ruins of which you can see from the canal. INSIDERTIP Mooney's (Main Street / tel. 045 52 53 60) is well worth a stop. This traditional Irish pub also serves as a shop for local residents. Ask whether they can make you up a cheddar cheese sandwich on brown bread. There is no menu but you can taste diverse types of whiskeys as well as the best Irish whiskey of the entire tour. From the medieval market town of ❸ Athy **our route on the River Barrow heads downriver** where 23 locks have to be overcome on the stretch to St Mullins. In ❹ Carlow look out for the ruined Norman castle on the eastern shore. **Via Muine Bheag, the river now carries on to ❺ Graiguenamanagh** in the Barrow Valley. You have to drop anchor here not just to grab a snapshot of Duiske Abbey, Ireland's oldest Cistercian monastery dating back to 1207, but also to enjoy a stroll around the picturesque medieval town. Visit Cushendale Woollen Mills (Mon–Fri 8.30am–5.30pm, Sat 10am–1pm / Mill Road / www.cushendale.ie), where

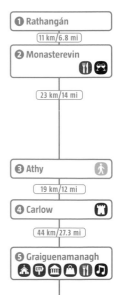

❶ Rathangán

11 km/6.8 mi

❷ Monasterevin

23 km/14 mi

❸ Athy

19 km/12 mi

❹ Carlow

44 km/27.3 mi

❺ Graiguenamanagh

| 9 km/5.6 mi |

6 St Mullins
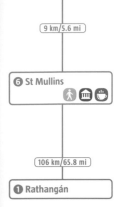

| 106 km/65.8 mi |

1 Rathangán

they have been weaving pretty blankets and clothing for many generations. The best dinner on this tour can be had at the **Waterside** *daily from 6.30pm | The Quay | tel. 059 9 72 42 46 | www.watersideguesthouse.com | Moderate)* on the riverside – INSIDER TIP often with live music in the evening, ranging from jazz to blues.

The journey ends in **6 St Mullins** at a lock, as the next section of the river to the estuary beyond is not suitable for light canal boats. Walk around the pleasant town of St Mullins before heading back. A restored storehouse from the 18th century now houses the INSIDER TIP **Mullíchain Café** *(Tue–Sun 11am–6pm | The Quay | tel. 051 42 44 40 | Budget)* with tables directly on the canal. If you've only booked your boat for one week, you'll have to turn round now in order to hand it back in good time in **1 Rathangán**, since the boats only go at speeds of 6–8 km/h (3.7–5 mph) and you need time at the locks.

Gently cruising from lock to lock along the canal

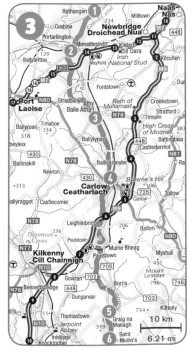

FROM DONEGAL THROUGH NORTHERN IRELAND TO BELFAST

START: ❶ Donegal
END: ❿ Belfast

2 days
Driving time
8 hours

Distance:
➡ 300 km/186 mi

COSTS: approx. 400 euros (hire car, petrol, accommodation, admission, food)

WHAT TO PACK: swimwear, sturdy hiking shoes, rain jacket, camera

IMPORTANT TIPS: Arrange with the rental car company to take the vehicle into Northern Ireland!

Don't forget that the currency in Northern Ireland is the Great Britain Pound; it can be changed in shops, at the money changer or in banks

Information available from: Belfast Visitor & Convention Bureau
(47 Donegall Square | tel. 028 90 23 90 26 | www.visit-belfast.com)

This tour takes you into Northern Ireland. The route goes from Donegal past Derry to the Giant's Causeway, the most famous attraction in Northern Ireland, and heads south along the coast to the capital city of Belfast.

Start your journey by car early morning from ❶ **Donegal** → p. 85. **Head to Strabane and from there to ❷ Derry/ Londonderry**. The **city walls** are the most fully intact within the United Kingdom and from the tower, you get amazing views over the town and the Foyle estuary. Built in the 17th century, the walls stand up to 8 m/26 ft high with seven gateways and stretch over 1.5 km/1 mi. You can walk along them between the hours of sunrise and sunset. While it is still morning, **continue your tour in the direction of Coleraine and then to Portrush** on the north coast. **A few kilometres to the east near the A2** you'll spot the ruins of an impressive 16th century castle perching on the steep coastal cliffs: ❸ **Dunluce Castle** *(April–Sept daily 10am–6pm, Oct–March 10am–4pm | admission 5 GBP)*, which offers spectacular coastal views and good hiking trails into the landscape around. Have you had enough fresh air for today? Then check into the ❹ **Royal Court House** *(18 rooms | 233 Ballybogey Road | Portrush | tel. 028 70 82 22 36 | www.royalcourthotel.co.uk | Moderate)* 2 km/1.2 mi away (back on the A2) ideal for an overnight stay. In the afternoon, visit the ❺ **Old Bushmills Distillery**

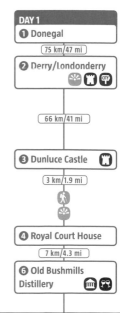

DAY 1

❶ Donegal

75 km/47 mi

❷ Derry/Londonderry

66 km/41 mi

❸ Dunluce Castle

3 km/1.9 mi

❹ Royal Court House

7 km/4.3 mi

❺ Old Bushmills Distillery

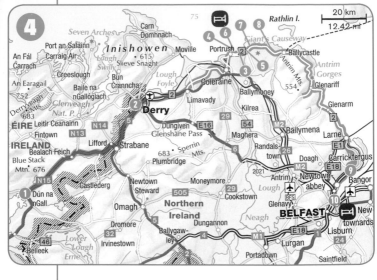

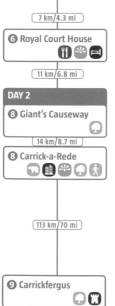

→ p. 86, nearby, a century-old whiskey distillery, before returning to the **6 Royal Court House** where you can enjoy INSIDER TIP fantastic views over the Atlantic from the hotel's restaurant.

Next morning, it's just a 10–15 minute car journey along the A2 coastal road to the 7 Giant's Causeway → p. 86. After two to three hours here, head to the nearby island **8 Carrick-a-Rede**, even longer detours would be worthwhile. The name of this miniature, uninhabited island literally translates as the 'rock of the casting'. The island is inhabited by puffins and eiders but is famous for its swinging rope bridge (even when the weather isn't stormy) which is maintained by the National Trust – the **Carrick-a-Rede Rope Bridge** *(March/April/Sept/Ot 9.30am–6pm, June– Aug 9.30am–7.30pm, Dec–Jan daily 9.30am–3.30pm | admission 5,90 GBP)* – is 30 m/98 ft high and spans over a 20 m/66 ft wide strait below. Although the rope bridge attracts many tourists in summer, this solitary bridge is most impressive on darker cloudy days. If you've had enough of windy adventures, your tour now takes you **further south along the coastal road 2** past **Ballycastle, Glenarriff** and the ferry town of **Larne** to **9 Carrickfergus**. The Irish folk song with the same name is world famous. Take a step back into medieval times in **Carrickfergus Castle** *(Easter–*

Sept daily 10am–6pm, Oct–Easter Mon–Sat 10am–4pm | admission 5 GBP) on the north banks of Belfast Lough.

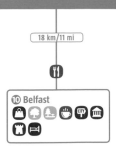

18 km/11 mi

⑩ Belfast

It's now just a short distance to ⑩ **Belfast**. Fill up your picnic hamper in one of the many small food shops. **Sawers Deli** *(7 College Street | Fountain Centre)* offers some of the best Irish delicatessens. Then spread out your picnic blanket in the public **Botanic Gardens** *(daily from 7.30am | Botanic Av. | College Park)*, a popular meeting point for lunch. If dark clouds threaten, take a 2 km/1.2 mi stroll to the **Crown Liquor Saloon** *(46 Great Victoria Street | www.nicholsonspubs.co.uk)* for a traditional Irish coffee. Do not miss the **City Hall** *(Donegall Square | guided tours: Mon–Fri 11am, 2pm, 3pm, Sat 2pm and 3pm)*, the hall in the centre of Belfast is a striking architectural construction which can be admired on the one-hour tours with free admission. **Belfast Castle** *(Sun/Mon 9am–6pm, Tue–Sat 9am–10pm | free admission | Antrim Road | www.belfastcastle.co.uk)* dating back to the 12th century has a turbulent past; today it serves as a museum, a popular place for weddings and a pleasant cafe. **Dukes At Queens** *(32 rooms | 65–67 University Street | Queens Quarter | tel. 028 90 23 66 66 | www.dukesatqueens.com | Moderate)* is recommended for accommodation, a boutique hotel with fantastic breakfasts.

Belfast City Hall: An ideal sightseeing spot on bad weather days

107

SPORTS & ACTIVITIES

Golfing, horseback riding and fishing – Ireland has always combined rural life and country sports; add to that trendy activities such as hang-gliding and diving.Like many other places, Ireland is also witnessing a boom in spa treatments. One particular speciality is its seaweed baths. Although they do not sound very appealing, they are in fact extremely relaxing and an excellent treatment for your skin, body and soul. On the west coast especially, the warm Atlantic waters and algae are supposed to promote sustainable health and well-being.

CANOE HIKING

Ireland's many lakes, rivers and canals are waiting to be paddled down, and even white-water rafting is possible. The most suitable rivers are the Liffey, Barrow, Shannon and Suir. Request the tourist board's *(www.discoverireland. com)* brochure on lakes and waterways. Information: *Canoeing Ireland, Sport HQ (National Sports Campus | Blanchardstown | Dublin 15 | tel. 01 6 25 11 05 | www. canoe.ie).*

CYCLING

Bike tours are especially popular in the scenic west and southwest. Rather than cycle paths, there are surfaced side roads with little traffic. Bikes can be hired nearly anywhere, e.g. at Shannon Airport by *Emerald Alpine (21 Roches Street | Limerick | tel. 061 41 69 83 | www.irelandrent*

A paradise for fishermen, golfers or horse-back riders. Wellness fans love relaxing in a seaweed bath

abike.com). Bikes can be handed back at other places as well.

DIVING

Irish waters offer good visibility of up to 30 m/98 ft. Flora (huge kelp forests) and fauna (from schools of herring to seals) are varied, and the Gulf Stream ensures bearable diving temperatures. The western side of the island has numerous wrecks, but the eastern coast too has interesting dive sites, accessible by boat.

Information for scuba divers from: *Irish Underwater Council (78A Patrick Street | Dun Laoghaire | Co. Dublin | tel. 01 2 84 46 01 | www.diving.ie).* A dive base with hire, service and accommodation is *Mevagh Dive Centre (Milford Road | Carrigart | Co. Donegal | tel. 074 9 15 47 08 | www.mevaghdiving.com).*

FISHING

Thousands of lakes, countless rivers and nearly 3220 km/2000 mi of coastline –

small wonder that nearly every Irish male from this area goes fishing here. Salmon populate the Atlantic rivers and trout live in most of the brooks and lakes *(game angling)*. *Coarse angling* for pike, eel and other fish is also popular. Licences can be purchased at the angling shops and tourist information centres.

At the ports of Galway, Kinsale, Valentia Island and Youghal, you can take part in deep-sea fishing expeditions. If you are into fly fishing, there are several hotels that offer fly-fishing packages *(www.fly fishing.com)*. Information: *Inland Fisheries Ireland (3044 Lake Drive | Dublin | tel. 01 2 78 70 22 | www.fisheriesireland.ie)*. For more information go to *www.fishing inireland.info*.

GOLFING

Ireland boasts 425 golf courses, some of them even offer spectacular views of the Atlantic. Golfing is a popular pastime here, so green fees are low. A golfing guide and a list of golfing holiday operators is published by the Irish tourist board on the website *www.discoverireland. ie/golf*. You'll also find small *pitch-and-putt* golf courses with fairways of 50–70 m/165–230 ft in nearly every village.

HANG GLIDING

With all these rolling hillsides, unspoilt bogs and the stead cool breeze coming in from the Atlantic, Ireland offers ideal conditions for *hang gliding*. The Wicklow mountains south of Dublin are a core area. Before starting out get information on the regulations by consulting the *Irish Hang Gliding and Paragliding Association (www.ihpa.ie)*. One recommended operator, also for beginners, is *Paraglide Adventure (tel. 01 8 30 38 84 | www. paraglideadventure.com)*.

HIKING

Many hiking trails have been laid out and signposted in scenic locations running across hills and along brooks, rivers and lakes. For descriptions of hiking trails in national parks see *www.npws.ie*. Hikes in the coastal periphery of Dublin with committed guides, e.g. onto Muck Rock, on Lambay Island and on the cliffs above Howth, are run by *www.howth guidedtours.com*. Guided circular hikes are available through *www.walkinghi kingireland.com* and *www.walktalkire land.com*. On *www.discoverireland.com* you will find lots of information on Ireland's most beautiful hiking trails.

HORSERIDING

The Irish landscape is perfect for horseback riding. A renowned operator is *Horse Holiday Farm (Mount Temple, Grange | Co. Sligo | tel. 071 9 16 61 52 |*

www.horseholidayfarm.net). For information on 16 places to spend an equestrian holiday and other activities on horseback, see *www.ehi.ie.* Trips on the 'Post-to-Post Trail Ride' are also offered.

SAILING

Nearly 3220 km/2000 mi of coastline, 100 yachting clubs and 50 marinas surround the Emerald Isle. The ideal sailing area lies on the southern coast between Waterford and Kinsale. For more information contact the *Irish Sailing Association (3 Park Road | Dun Laoghaire | Co. Dublin | tel. 01 2 80 02 39 | www.sail ing.ie)*.

SURFING

Offshore winds and spectacular swells: Ireland's north-westerly coast offers fantastic surfing conditions. The resorts of Bundoran, Tullan and Enniscrone have become the most popular meeting points for the surfer crowd. Surfing championships have been repeatedly held in Bundoran (www.bundoransurf co.com). This is not a sport for the faint-hearted though as in the main season between autumn and spring conditions are often stormy and rainy. Wetsuits are essential to fight off the cold water temperatures.

WELLBEING

Bathing in seaweed: 100 years ago, Ireland had around 300 baths where you could go to bathe in the Atlantic water and seaweed to relax your muscles, increase your blood circulation and rejuvenate your skin. Most of these baths closed down over the years yet some have survived and have re-opened while other new baths have been built. These seaweed baths can be found on Ireland's west coast.

Plunge in the water: Even beginners can learn kayaking on the Killary Fjord near Connemara

TRAVEL WITH KIDS

Whether it's organised leisure time in a theme park or crabbing on their own at the seaside: far from the buzz of the city, children are welcomed with open arms in green Ireland.

IN AND AROUND DUBLIN

INSIDER TIP **THE ARK** (U B4) (*m b4*)

At the *Cultural Centre Ark*, toddlers are already encouraged to experiment with paints, wool and other materials to create objects of art that are then exhibited in the gallery. There are also theatre performances, shows and workshops. Reservations recommended. *Mon–Fri 10am–5pm | admission from 10 euros | 11a Eustace Street | Temple Bar | Dublin 2 | www.ark.ie*

INSIDER TIP **GREENAN FARM MUSEUMS & MAZE**
(139 F5–6) (*m K12*)

A visit to Greenan Maze makes any day a pleasant one. Not only will you learn a lot, you'll have a lot of fun too! There's plenty to do on both sunny and rainy days since the complex is both inside and outside. They have an inviting farm with many animals and a farmhouse museum located in a 16th-century farm building. The labyrinth is even difficult for adults to solve. Crafts as well as fresh *scones* and pastries are available from the tearoom. *April/May/Sep Sat/Sun 10am–6pm, June–Aug daily 10am–6pm | adult admission 8, children 7, family price 28 euros | Ballinanty | at Greenan, Rathdrum | Co. Wicklow | www.greenanmaze.com*

Child-friendly Ireland: the Emerald Isle has the youngest population in Europe – families everywhere can expect a sincere welcome

IMAGINOSITY (135 E4) (🔲 K11)

In this interactive facility (Dublin Children Museum) there are models and installations, allowing children up to nine years of age to give free rein to their imagination and creativity: building, painting, climbing and acting. *Mon 1.30–5.30pm, Tue–Fri 9.30am–5.30pm, Sat/Sun 10am–6pm | admission adults and children 8 euros | The Plaza, Beacon South Quarter | Sandyford | LUAS tram to Stillorgan | buses 114/75/46B and 11A to Blackthorn Drive | www.imaginosity.ie*

NATIONAL LEPRECHAUN MUSEUM (U B3) (🔲 b3)

Welcome to the world of elves, fairies and leprechauns. Take a 45-minute tour through the empire of Ireland's mythology. You'll take an interactive journey and discover the sounds, sights, stories and magic of mythical Ireland, home of the leprechaun. Even the critical Irish Times were impressed. *Daily 10am–6.30pm | adult admission 14, children 10 euros | Twilfit House | 1 Jervis Street | Dublin | www.leprechaunmuseum.ie*

THE SOUTH

AQUA DOME (136 C3) (*𝄞 C15*)
Large waterworld leisure complex with various slides, waves, pools and boats; also minigolf and different games. *Wet, wild & wonderful. Mon–Fri 10am–10pm, Sat/Sun 10am–9pm | adult admission 15, children 12 euros | Dan Spring Road | at the Dingle Road Junction in the south of town on the River Lee | Tralee | Co. Kerry | www.aquadome.ie*

FOTA WILDLIFE PARK (138 A6) (*𝄞 F16*)
The wildlife park shelters some 90 kinds of animals in outdoor enclosures, amongst them giraffes and cheetahs. Children enjoy the daily feeding session in the early morning and late afternoon. *Daily 10am–4.30pm | adult admission 16, children 10.50, families 48 euros | Fota Island | at Carrigtwohill (near Cork) | www.fota wildlife.ie*

INSIDERTIP **SEAFARI** (136 C4) (*𝄞 C16*)
Be sure to pack a warm jacket cause you'll be heading to the sea! Take a boat trip and do some seal watching on the Kenmare River and in Kenmare Bay. It takes two hours. Over 150 animals live off the coast here, and you're guaranteed to see some during this tour. You'll also learn a lot of interesting facts about these animals. *April–Oct, tours are dependent on the tides | adult trips 25, children (12–15 yrs) 15, (under 12) 12.50 euros | 3 Pier Road | Kenmare | tel. 064 6642059 | www.sea fariireland.com*

VALENTIA HARBOUR TOURS (136 A–B4) (*𝄞 A–B16*)
A special amphibian vehicle – a large boat on three wheels – can take up to 48 passengers on a fun harbour tour between Valentia Island and the mainland. On the trip you'll pass ruined ring forts, monastic settlements and the port of Knightstown, while seals loll about on small rocky islets. *Duration of the trip 2.5 hrs | adults 15, children 10 euros | Cahersiveen | Ring of Kerry | tel. 087 2854859 | www.valentia harbourtours.com*

Boys surfing in Kilkee: Sometimes happiness is a small board

THE WEST COAST

GALWAY ATLANTAQUARIA, NATIONAL AQUARIUM OF IRELAND
(132 C4) (*D11*)

Fish and other sea creatures inhabit 2000 m²/2392 yd of a natural-looking universe. The lighthousereplica houses a café, and in the submarine visitors can experience a simulated diving expedition. *Daily 10am–5pm (Oct–Feb closed Mon/Tue) | adult admission 12, children 7.50 euros | The Promenade | Salthill | Galway | www.nationalaquarium.ie*

DOLPHINWATCH (136 C1) (*C14*)

The Shannon estuary shelters a colony of dolphins, which can be visited on two-hour boat tours. *Tours April–Sept | adults 35, children 20 euros | Kilcredaun | near Carrigaholt (60 km/37 mi west of Ennis) | Co. Clare | tel. 065 9 05 8156 | www.dolphinwatch.ie*

LAHINCH SEAWORLD & LEISURE CENTRE (132 C5) (*C13*)

A mix of play and climbing area, swimming pool and splash pool, jacuzzi, sauna and aquarium: entertainment for the entire day. *Mon–Wed 7am–9.30pm, Thu/Fri 9am–9pm, Sat/Sun 10am–8pm | adult admission 7–10, children 5.50 euros | The Promenade | Lahinch | Co. Clare | www.lahinchseaworld.com*

OCEAN WORLD MARA BEO
(136 B3) (*B15*)

Penguins, seals and sharks in Ireland's biggest aquarium. And a *Kids Zone*! *Daily 10am–5pm | adult admission 13.50, children 8.75, families 38 euros | The Wood | Dingle Town | www.dingle-oceanworld.ie*

THE MIDLANDS

FETHARD FOLK, FARM AND TRANSPORT MUSEUM (138 C3) (*G14*)

City kids can learn a lot about rural life here: the old railway station at the edge of Fethard shows 1200 objects, amongst them many historic means of transportation and vehicles such as carriages and prams. There's a play area for children too. *May–Oct daily 10am–6pm | admission farm area 2 euros, museum 3 euros | Cashel Road | R 692 | Fethard | Co. Tipperary | www.fethard.com*

PARSONS GREEN PARK AND PET FARM (138 B4) (*F15*)

Here children and adults may visit riverside gardens, a farm museum and an animal enclosure. Or do you prefer to sit in the Viking Sweat House? Sporty types can go pony-riding, take a boat tour on the river, or try a round of tennis, basketball or crazy golf with many unusual obstacles. If you want to stay longer, stay on the campsite or rent an apartment. *April–Sept daily 10am–8pm | admission adults 4, children 3, families 15 euros | Clogheen | Co. South Tipperary | www.clogheen.com*

FESTIVALS & EVENTS

Summer on the Emerald Isle is accompanied by events and festivals. Some of them – such as the Cork Jazz Festival – are internationally known. The *fleadh* festivals are exclusively dedicated to traditional music – dancing allowed! Every village has its own festival. A calendar of festivals & events is available from the Irish Tourist Board.

FESTIVALS & EVENTS

JANUARY
INSIDER TIP *Temple Bar Traditional Festival of Irish Music:* a five-day session in late January for folk musicians on the fiddle, bodhrán and banjo. *www.templebartrad.com*

MARCH
★ ● *St Patrick's Festival,* mid-March: around the national holiday, all of Dublin parties for five days, with parades, dance, acrobatics. *www.stpatricksfestival.ie*

JUNE
Bloomsday, 16 June: one day in the life of Leopold Bloom in 1904, described in vast detail by James Joyce in his monumental novel 'Ulysses'. That fateful day is repeated for his followers in lectures, walks and visits to the pub. *Dublin | www.jamesjoyce.ie*

JULY
Galway Arts Festival, second half of the month: two weeks of arts, theatre, dance, music, comedy, literature and film. *Tel. 091 50 97 00 | www.giaf.ie*

AUGUST
Kilkenny Arts Festival, ten days in mid-August: arts and music festival ranging from cathedral concerts to street theatre. *Tel. 056 776 36 63 | www.kilkennyarts.ie*
● **INSIDER TIP** *Fleadh Cheoil na hEireann*, second half of the month: one week of Irish folk music – in pubs, hotels and schools, even on the street. Every year the fleadh takes place in a different town. *www.comhaltas.com*
Dublin Horse Show, for five days horses take centre stage: dressage and jumping competitions, horse shows and a major horse fair. *www.dublinhorseshow.com*
Puck Fair, three days mid-month: authentic rural fair with lots of music, cattle and horse fair and 100,000 visitors. The action revolves around a male goat, the puck. *Tel. 066 9 76 23 66 | Killorglin | Co. Kerry | www.puckfair.ie*

Music and dancing form the main ingredients of Irish celebrations – especially the highlight of the calendar: St Patrick's Day, the national holiday

Rose of Tralee International Festival, five days: beauty contest for young Irish women with plenty of open-air concerts. *Tel. 066 712 13 22 | Tralee | www.roseof tralee.ie*

SEPTEMBER

Galway Oyster & Seafood Festival: three-day gourmet festival featuring fresh fish, lots of Guinness and oysters. *www.gal wayoysterfest.com*

Dublin Fringe Festival, two weeks: 300 events on 40 stages – theatre, dance, comedy, music, artistry. One evening: **INSIDER TIP** Dublin Culture Night *(www.culturenight.ie)* with 150 participating culture institutions. *www.fringefest.com*

OCTOBER

Kinsale Gourmet Festival, three days of culinary events in Kinsale. *www.kinsale restaurants.com*

Guinness Jazz Festival, four days in Cork: legendary event with jazz greats from all over the world. *www.corkjazzfestival.com*

Wexford Festival Opera, second half of Oct: forgotten and little-known operas. *Wexford | www.wexfordopera.com*

NATIONAL HOLIDAYS

1 Jan	New Year's Day
17 March	*St Patrick's Day* (national holiday)
19 April 2019/20 April 2020	Good Friday
21, 22 April 2019/12, 13 April 2020	Easter
1st Monday in May	May Day
1st Monday in June	Bank holiday
1st Monday in Aug	Bank holiday
Last Monday in Oct	Bank holiday
25 Dec	Christmas
26 Dec	*St Stephen's Day*

LINKS, BLOGS, APPS & MORE

LINKS & BLOGS

www.heritageireland.ie Everything you need to know about the country's cultural history and historic buildings

www.discoverireland.ie The website keeps you up to date on – among other things – the countless events and festivals taking place on the island, the Festival of the Erne in Belturbet for instance, that you'd have been unlikely to hear about otherwise

www.ireland-fun-facts.com Readable collection of curiosities, plus unusual travel ideas

www.thephoenix.ie The homepage of the Irish satirical magazine inspired by Private Eye allows you to view an entire recent edition, pulling the rug from under political, social and assorted posturing

www.mythicalireland.com The website reveals the secret and mythical side of the Emerald Isle: the holy stones and ritual sites of the megalithic period

www.lovindublin.com Very inviting website listing events and especially restaurants (categories include 'posh' and 'hipster') in Dublin. Also has a recipe section

abigblogofirishliterature.blogspot.com Everything about Irish literature, from James Joye to Colum McCann

www.irelands-hidden-gems.com Blog by Irish travel writer Susan Byron, a vast source of information on everything Irish. Great on lists, from the 10 best museums to Irish lighthouses

www.irishcentral.com American website catering for the many million Irish expats or people of Irish descent living in the US. News, politics and culture from Ireland, as well as travel tips especially for Americans

Regardless of whether you are still researching your trip or already in Ireland: these addresses will provide you with more information, videos and Networksss to make your holiday even more enjoyable

VIDEOS & MUSIC

twitter.com/Ireland This community is mainly interested in the arts and culture

www.youtube.com/watch?v=OcdOvseiCoc Short clip with beautiful aerial footage of Ireland in HD

www.youtube.com/watch?v=py3cvo1vqSE Short atmospheric clip showing St Patrick's day celebrations in Dublin – to get you into the mood

www.thisisirishfilm.ie/ The Irish Film Board's media hub is a great showcase of fillums

www.visitdublin.com Want to discover Dublin on foot? Download audioguides and walks as podcasts

APPS

Around Me At a click, this programme by Tweakersoft reveals what's around you: cafés, restaurants, cinemas, theatre, hotels etc., with city map and distances

Dublin Bus Type in your destination or bus route to receive the departure times (including the last bus!) on your iPhone

Visit Dublin App This useful app for iPhone and Android uses 'camera view' and 'guide me' to lead you to sights, hotels and restaurants.

Ireland's Blue Book This free app offers geographical guides to classy manor houses, castles and country estates

Journey Planner App by www.transportforireland.ie leading to buses and trains, ferrys and taxis – maps, routes, timetables for iPhone and Android

Wild Atlantic Way A beautifully designed app full of tips and sites in case you fancy a roadtrip on Ireland's ultimate route of the westcoast

iGuide Dublin A free, yet well-designed app giving information on shopping, (new) restaurants, other sites and today's news

TRAVEL TIPS

ACCOMMODATION

Sadly, the quality of accommodation in Ireland often doesn't quite correlate with the price. This is especially true when it comes to booking the mid-range hotels in Ireland which are often overpriced. You are better off booking everything online before your holiday. This way, you'll always find the best offers and prices.

The tourist board will send lists of inspected bed & breakfast places, as well as holiday cottages and apartments. On the face of it, the cheapest choice after hostels are B&Bs. In towns, the price per person ranges between 40 and 55 euros, depending on the level of comfort: *www.bandbireland.com*.

In high season, holiday apartments cost from 300 euros upwards, holiday cottages from 600 euros per week. Information and booking e.g. at: *Irish Cottage Holiday Homes (Bracken Court | Bracken Road | Sandyford | Dublin 18 | tel. 01 2 05 27 77 | www.irishcottageholidays.com)*.

RESPONSIBLE TRAVEL

It doesn't take a lot to be environmentally friendly whilst travelling. Don't just think about your carbon footprint whilst flying to and from your holiday destination but also about how you can protect nature and culture abroad. As a tourist it is especially important to respect nature, look out for local products, cycle instead of driving, save water and much more. If you would like to find out more about eco-tourism please visit: *www.ecotourism.org*

The websites *www.hiddenireland.com* and *www.irelands-blue-book.ie* lead you to small but beautiful accommodation choices. For a list of exclusive hotels housed in former castles and manor houses contact *Ireland's Blue Book (63 Fitzwilliam Square | Dublin 2 | tel. 01 6 76 99 14)* or see *www.manorhousehotels.com* (all *Expensive*).

A selection of country hotels is available at *www.irishcountryhotels.com*. A search engine for hotels (incl. special offers) is *www.hotelsireland.com*.

For holidays on a farm: *Irish Farmhouse Holidays (Belleek Road | Ballyshannon | Co. Donegal | tel. 071 9 82 22 22 | www.irish farmholidays.com)*.

Unusual accommodation such as a lighthouse or a castle can be booked through *The Irish Landmark Trust (11 Parnell Square | Dublin 2 | tel. 01 6 70 47 33 | www.irishlandmark.com)*.

ARRIVAL

Ferry routes from Britain are Holyhead-Dun Laoghaire and Liverpool-Dublin (www.poferries.com), Fishguard or Pembroke to Rosslare and Stranraer to Belfast (www.stenaline.co.uk); the Swansea to Cork route (*www.fastnetonline.com*) is again in doubt, but there's a new Liverpool to Belfast route (www.stenaline.co.uk). Look for special offers on fare-comparing sites such as www.ferriestoireland.net or www.cheapferry.co.uk.

The famous budget carrier Ryanair *(www.ryanair.com)* flies from London to Dublin and Kerry. Air France has services from New York to Dublin via Paris. The state carrier Aer Lingus *(www.aerlin*

From arrival to weather

**Your holiday from start to finish:
the most important addresses and information for your Ireland trip**

gus.com) has turned itself into a low-cost airline, offering direct flights from New York to Dublin and Shannon (an airport handy for the west, but with decreasing traffic these days) and from Boston, Chicago and Orlando to Dublin. Connections within Ireland are offered by Aer Arann *(www.aerarann.com)*. From Dublin airport to the city centre, the scheduled buses no. 41 and 102 (3.30 euros) take up to 45 min., with a lot of stops, express buses no. 747 and no. 748 (6 euros, Airlink) approx. 20–30 min.; at night, the bus 41n can take you into the city centre and to the railway stations (6.50 euros). A taxi from the airport to the centre costs around 20–25 euros, approx. 15–25 min.

BANKS & CREDIT CARDS

Opening times of the banks: *Mon–Fri 10am–12.30pm and 1.30–3pm or until 5pm.* Cashpoints are available in towns and most larger villages; they take debit and credit cards. Credit cards are widely accepted.

BATHING & BEACHES

Ireland's beaches are among the cleanest in Europe and dozens have been certified with the Blue Flag (for their water quality). Yet even during the hottest days in summer, the Atlantic waters are still pretty cold (14–17 degrees). Dubliners take the DART suburban railway to the bathing resort of Bray, 20 km/12.5 mi south of the capital; however if fish and chip shops and arcades are not really for you, stay on the train for another two stops until you reach Killiney and its natural pebble beach. If you're looking for

sandy beaches and dramatic coastline, head for Achill Island, the bathing resort of Waterville on the Iveragh peninsula and its tourist infrastructure.

CAMPING

Ireland has more than 200 officially recognised campsites. Get the 'Caravan, Camping & Motorhome Guide' at *www.camping-ireland.ie.* Small camper vans, also called *bunk campers* here, as they feature two or four bunk beds, have no bath-

CURRENCY CONVERTER

£	€	€	£
1	1.15	1	0.85
3	3.40	3	2.65
5	5.70	5	4.40
13	17.70	13	11.50
40	45	40	35
75	85	75	66
120	136	120	106
250	283	250	220
500	565	500	440

$	€	€	$
1	0.80	1	1.20
3	2.40	3	3.70
5	4	5	6.20
13	10.50	13	16
40	32.50	40	50
75	60	75	92
120	97	120	148
250	200	250	310
500	405	500	615

For current exchange rates see www.xe.com

room, shower or WC, but do have a kitchenette and fridge. For rental, contact *Bunk Campers (in summer: 100 euros per day with two, 140 euros with four beds | www. bunkcampers.com)*.

CAR HIRE

To hire a car you have to be at least 25. A national driving licence in English is sufficient. A car costs from 35 euros per day. To avoid high charges at pickup , book your car (with fully comprehensive insurance) before you travel. **INSIDERTIP** Order a small car for manoeuvring around the narrow lanes and regional roads.

CLIMATE, WHEN TO GO

The Irish have 'lots of weather', meaning that rain and sunshine alternate several times a day. That's why there is no bad weather, there's only inappropiate clothing. In winter temperatures hardly ever fall below 0 °C/32 °F. Summer temperatures then rarely inch over the 25 °C/77 °F mark. Rain is always on the cards, particularly in the west. May and June are the sunniest months, while July and August are the high season for tourism.

CONSULATES & EMBASSIES

UK EMBASSY
29 Merrion Road | Ballsbridge | Dublin 4 | tel. 01 250 37 00 | www.britishembassy inireland.fco.gov.uk
US EMBASSY
42 Elgin Road | Ballsbridge | Dublin 4 | tel. 01 6 68 87 77 | http://dublin.usembassy.gov

CUSTOMS

Within the European Union, EU citizens over 18 may freely import and export goods for personal use, e. g. 800 cigarettes, 90 litres of wine and 10 litres of spirits per person. North American citizens are subject to much lower allowances, including only 200 cigarettes and 1 litre of spirits. Personal defence sprays etc. are illegal in Ireland. For accessibly presented information, see *www.citizens information.ie*

DRIVING

Ireland, like the UK, drives on the left. Roundabouts have right of way. Top speed in built-up areas is 50 km/h (31 mph), on country roads 100 km/h (62 mph). Regional country roads are often quite narrow. The drink-driving limit is at 0.5. EU citizens only need their national or European licence. North American licences are accepted too. WARNING: Fines (e. g. for drink-driving, speeding, parking offences) are very high, and drink-driving over the limit will set you back at least 1270 euros! On some sections of the motorway (e.g. A 50, the ring around Dublin) a toll must be paid. Some car rental agencies charge your credit card afterwards (ask at booking!). You can otherwise pay the toll (if there is one!) or at one of 2000 pay stations *(www.payzone.ie)*.

DISCOUNTS FOR TOURISTS

For 40 euros, the *Heritage Card (www. heritageireland.ie)* gives you free access to 100 heritage sites for one year.

ELECTRICITY

Voltage: 220 volts; British appliances work without adapters; North Americans need to bring a US two-to-three pin adapter.

EMERGENCY

Nationwide emergency number: *999* or *112*

HEALTH

Chemists or pharmacies are often attached to a drugstore. Information on emergency pharmacies is posted in the window of drugstores.

British citizens should bring their EHIC (European Health Insurance Card) or a replacement certificate, which entitles you to free emergency treatment at hospitals, GPs' surgeries and dentists.

HORSE DRAWN CARAVANS

Horse drawn caravans are available for up to four people and can be hired near Dublin from *Clissmann Horse Caravans (Cronybyrne | Rathdrum | Co. Wicklow | tel. 0404 46920 | www.clissmannhorse caravans.com)*. The tourist information office can provide you with other addresses in the counties of Galway, Mayo and Wicklow. Caravan prices start from 900 (July/Aug. 1200) euros a week.

HOSTELS

Of the two dozen youth hostels grouped together in the *Irish Youth Hostel Association – An Oige*, more than half of them are open all year round. There is no age limit to book a room and an overnight stay will only cost you between 15–30 euros. For a list of hostels, contact the *Irish Youth Hostel Association (61 Mountjoy Street, Dublin 7 | tel. 01 8 30 45 55 | www. anoige.ie)*. There are also about 45 independent hostels (from 12 euros) listed in the *Guide to independent Holiday Hostels,* available from *Independent Hostels.* Book online at *www.hostels-ireland.com.*

IMMIGRATION

UK citizens need a valid passport or UK/Irish driving licence – the latter is only sufficient if you were born in the UK or Ireland before 1983. North American citizens require a passport but no visa for a holiday.

INFORMATION

IRELAND INFORMATION
UK: *103 Wigmore St | London W1U 1QS | tel. 0207 518 0800 | www.discoverire land.com/gb*
US: *345 Park Avenue | 17th Floor / New York, NY 10154, USA | tel. 0212 418 0800 | www.discoverireland.com/us*
Alongside the official tourist board website *www.discoverireland.com,* another good source of information before starting out is *www.ceolas.org/IrishNet*; this website provides you with links to all of the Irish and Irish-interest sites published all over the world.

BUDGETING

Guinness	£3.60–£4.50/$4.60–$4.70 *for a pint*
Cream tea	£4.50/$4.70 *for scones and tea*
Coffee	£2.70–£3.10/$3.45–$4 *for a cup*
Bus ticket	£14/$18 *for a single from Dublin to Cork*
Petrol	approx. £1.30/$1.70 *for a litre of plus unleaded*
Lunch	£8–£10.80/$10.30–$13.80 *for a pub lunch*
Oysters	£8/$10.30 *for six Galway oysters*

LANGUAGE

In the west, northwest and on the islands you'll hear a smattering of Irish, the language of the ancient Celts, alongside English. Road signs are bilingual.

NARROWBOATS / CABIN CRUISERS

Narrowboats are available in all sizes (with two to eight beds including a toilet, shower and kitchen), with bicycles and dinghies. You can even hire motor boats. No boating licence is needed as you are given an induction beforehand. You should expect to pay between 1500–2000 euros per week during the high season for a boat which can sleep up to four persons. You can hire boats from e.g. *Carrick Craft (3–9 Fairgreen Road/Unit 4 | Market Hill BT60 1PW | County Armagh | Nordirland | tel. 0044 28 38 34 49 93 | www.cruiseireland.com)*. Boats can be collected and returned in Banagher, Carrick-on-Shannon or Tully Bay (one-way tours are also available). For tours on the Grand Canal: *Canalways Ireland Barge Holidays (Spencer Bridge | Rathangán | Co. Kildare | tel. 087 2 34 38 79 | www.canalways.ie)*

PRICES

While the recession has lead to a decline in business in Ireland too, and thus to slightly lower prices, living costs remain very high on the island, making a holiday in Ireland not perfect in this sense. Dublin in particular is expensive. Even a simple pizza or pasta dish can set you back nearly 20 euros, a small soup with bread costs 10 euros in a restaurant. Within Europe, prices for groceries are only higher in Denmark. Apart from hostels, accommodation is also expensive compared to other European countries. It's worth planning ahead!

PUBLIC TRANSPORT

Bus Éireann (www.buseireann.ie) offers an *Open Road Pass*. You have a few options when purchasing this ticket. You can buy a ticket that's valid on three days duing a 6 days timeframe for 60 euros; a ticekt that's valid on 4 out of 8 days for 76.50 euros; or a ticket that's valid for 5 out of 10 days 93 euros. Dublin and other large towns offer a great public transport system; *Dublin Area Rapid Transport (DART)* offers travel along the coast. The *Iarnród Éireann (www.irishrail.ie)* offers train travel; the *Trekker Four Day Ticket* allows travellers to travel by Irish Rail for four consecutive days for 110 euros. *The Irish Explorer Rail Only Ticket* costs only 160 euros and offers customers 5 days unlimited train travel within a 15-day timeframe. For Children up to 16 years old, you'll only pay half price. Both tickets can only be purchased in Ireland and from ticket office.

PHONE & MOBILE PHONE

The country code for Ireland is: *00353*, UK: *0044*, USA/Canada *001*. Card phones can be purchased virtually anywhere and bought for 10, 15 or 20 euros. You can pick them up at any post office. Although it's true that there aren't any mobile roaming fees between EU countries anymore, by no means does this mean you'll have the same flat rate when using your phone on an Irish network. It is therefore a good idea to check the conditions listed in your contract before using a mobile internet connection in Ireland. Do it before your journey. Irish mobiles/cells operate on GSM standard. Interceptors are used in public buildings (including theatres) to switch off mobile phones.

TIME

Ireland runs on GMT Western European time, like the UK.

TIPPING

Taxi fares should be rounded up. In restaurants, it's fine to give a tip of around 10 per cent if it hasn't already been added to the bill). The same rule applies in pubs, but not at the bar. The hotel maids usually get 1 euro per day.

WEIGHTS & MEASURES

Despite Ireland's switch to the decimal system, you'll often find the imperial weight and measures still used:

1 foot (12 inches):	30.5 cm
1 gallon (8 pints):	4.48 l
1 inch:	2.54 cm
1 mile:	1.609 km
1 pint:	0.56 l
1 pound:	453 g
1 yard (3 feet):	91.4 cm

WIFI & INTERNET

Countless shopping malls, restaurants, coffeeshops and hotels offer free wireless internet access. Internet cafés are available in all larger towns: *www.cyber cafes.com*.

WEATHER IN DUBLIN

	Jan	Feb	March	April	May	June	July	Aug	Sept	Oct	Nov	Dec
Daytime temperatures in °C/°F	8/46	8/46	10/50	12/54	15/59	18/64	20/68	19/66	17/63	14/57	10/50	8/46
Nighttime temperatures in °C/°F	2/36	2/36	2/36	3/37	6/43	9/48	11/52	10/50	9/48	6/43	3/37	2/36
☀ Sunshine hours/day	2	3	4	6	7	7	6	5	4	3	2	2
☂ Precipitation days/month	13	11	10	11	11	11	13	13	12	12	12	13
≋ Water temperature in °C/°F	9/48	8/46	7/45	8/46	9/48	11/52	13/55	14/57	14/57	13/55	12/54	10/50

ROAD ATLAS

The green line indicates the Discovery Tour 'Ireland at a Glance'
The blue line indicates the other Discovery Tours

All tours are also marked on the pull-out map

Photo: A rocky bay in Baltimore

Exploring Ireland

The map on the back cover shows how
the area has been sub-divided

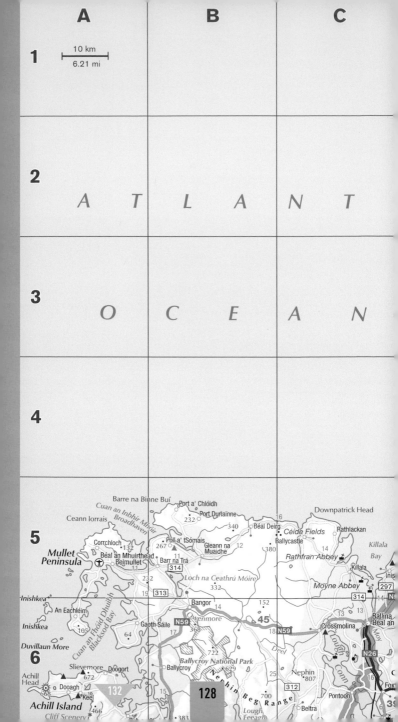

	A	**B**	**C**
1	10 km 6.21 mi		
2	*A T L A N T*		
3	*O C E A N*		
4			

5

A T L A N T I C

Barre na Binne Buí
Port a' Chlóidh
Port Durlainne
Downpatrick Head

Cuan an Inbhir Mhóir
Broadhaven

232

16

Ceann Iorrais
340
Béal Deirg
Céide Fields
Rathlackan

Corrchloch
132
Póll a' tSómais
267
Gleann na Muaidhe
12
Ballycastle
Killala
Bay

Mullet
Peninsula
Béal an Mhuirthead
Belmullet
11
Barr na Trá
380
Rathfran Abbey
14
Killala

314

Inis

1.1

Inishkea
232
Loch na Ceathrú Móire
332
Moyne Abbey
297

313

19

314

N

Bangor
152
Ballina
Béal an

14

45

13
13

An Eachléin
Glenmore
N59
18
N59

Inishkea
105
Gaoth Sáile
368
Crossmolina
N26

Cuan an Fhóid Dhuibh
Blacksod Bay
64
17

Deel

6

Duvillaun More

722
Ballycroy National Park
699
Nephin
807

Slievemore
672
Doogort
Ballycroy
25
312

Achill
Head
Dooagh
15
128
700
Pontoon
Fox

668
Keel

Nephin Beg Range

31

Achill Island
466
Cliff Scenery

Lough
Feeagh
Beltra

132

383

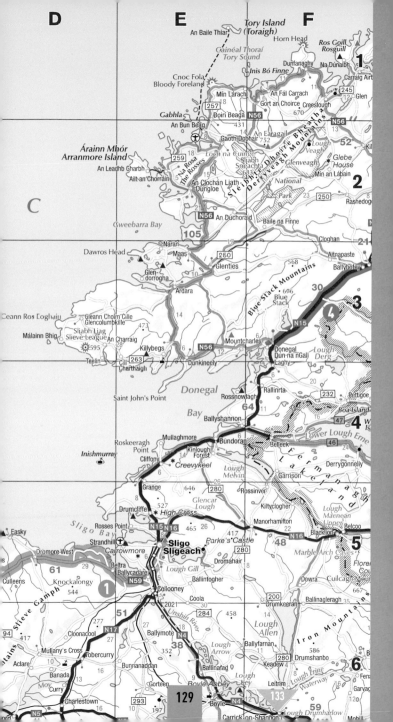

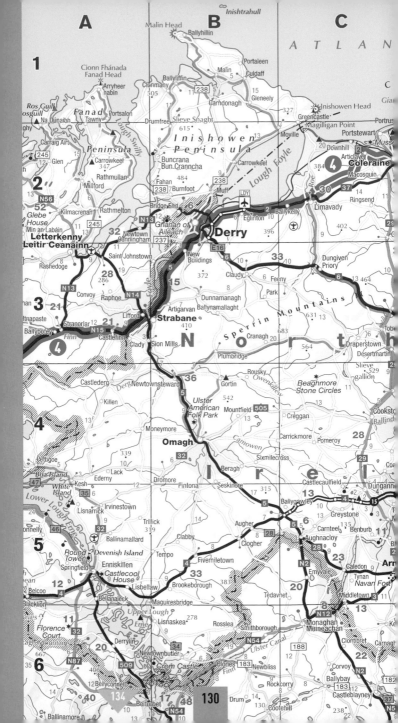

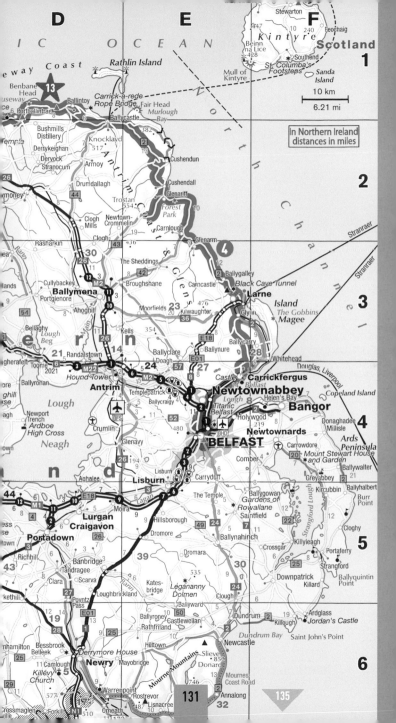

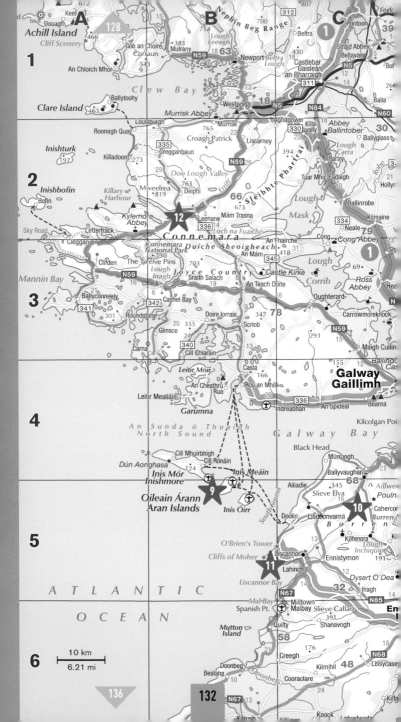